D1477591

The Bluebird Will Sing Tomorrow

Everyday a bird sings a new song in our lives...somedays the song may be melancholy or out of tune, and yet again another day, it will be a song of joy and delight in perfect pitch. No matter the tune, our hearts know that each tomorrow will have its own song meant just for us with its up and down notes. Whatever the song of the day might be, let us forever rejoice in its melody, remembering ... keep within your heart a green bough and a bluebird will come singing to stay.

Sr. Celine Steinberger, SNJM

The Bluebird Will Sing Tomorrow

Memoirs of Velma V. Morrison

As told to Kitty Delorey Fleischman

Additional Copies:
Contact
Harry W. Morrison Foundation
827 E. Park Blvd., Suite 200
Boise, Idaho 83706

iv

To our families…

*From Velma with love to my extended
family of EmKayans*

*From Kitty with love to all of my family…
especially my wonderful husband, the redhead
who brought me to Idaho, taught me to love it,
and twice has risked everything to
grubstake my businesses.*

Please note: These memoirs were composed from Velma's memories, without the help of any diaries or journals. Every effort has been made to keep events within the proper time frames. Many thanks are due to Fred Norman, friends who helped with proofreading and suggestions, and the staffs of the Harry W. Morrison Foundation, and *IDAHO magazine.* Special thanks and recognition are due to the Boise Public Library's Reference Desk for its invaluable help in nailing down newspaper clippings, stray details and photos.

Contents

ix Introduction

1 Child of the Great Depression

17 The Greatest Joys

35 The Wild Harvest

45 As God is my Witness

57 The Broiler

65 A New Life Calls

73 Mr. Morrison

93 A Wedding, a Honeymoon, and Boise

109 Horsing Around

125 Married Life

143 Single Again

151 The Legacy

171 A Mother's Tears

189 Corporate Suicide

199 Friends

213 The Bluebird Will Sing Tomorrow

221 Scrapbook

INTRODUCTION

The cover samples for this book are on the table in front of us, fanned out from the brass stud that holds them together. The colors are mostly either dark and rich, or neutral shades. One color stands out among them. It's a bright blue against the field of deep shades and non-colors. In previewing the cover possibilities, it is the one which struck me as being most appropriate for the petite and charming woman who sits now and studies them.

It seems odd to be choosing the cover before the first words for the book have been written, but at eighty-two, Velma Morrison is eager to get started on the project, and we both are eager to have it completed. Nothing about her suggests a penchant for putting things off until later.

"That color," says Velma. To my satisfaction, she is pointing to the bright blue. "I already have a title for my book. I've had the title picked out for years, and that fits it perfectly."

"What is the title?" I ask.

She eyes me with a twinkle and asks if I can guess. I have no ideas.

"I want to call it 'The Bluebird Will Sing Tomorrow,'" she says and asks if I know why. I think for a moment of the tidbits of her life I

know at the present. My first thought is related to the "bluebird of happiness" and how elusive it can be. She grew up in hard times under difficult circumstances. Divorce was uncommon in those days, but her parents split up when she was very young and her father reared the couple's three children.

As a child, she learned to work hard on the family's farm. She has had a lifetime of hard work. It has kept her mind sharp and active, and she has an avid interest in an amazingly broad range of topics. Hard work is a habit she still practices at an age when most of her contemporaries are tackling nothing more strenuous than an occasional game of bridge or lunch with friends. She still directs the work of the Morrison Foundation, is an active member on a number of boards, manages the family ranch on which she grew up, keeps up with family and her many friends, entertains frequently and still finds time to cook dinner for herself and her husband, John Hockberger.

Well known for her philanthropic work, Velma Morrison has kept a relatively low profile in the community, and little about her life seems to be common knowledge. In conducting a quick survey among friends as we were starting this project, I discovered virtually no accurate information about her life before or after she came to Boise in the late 1950s.

As it turns out, her sense of adventure and her fearless approach to life made her early years at least as interesting as the job she had as the wife of Harry Morrison, founder of Morrison-Knudsen, the largest, most prestigious engineering firm in the world at that time. She assumed that role at the age of thirty-eight, in an era where being a corporate wife was more of a career than a mere title.

There are many things about this fascinating woman that have received little or no attention. In our first weeks working together, I've heard about her working as a public health nurse in northwestern Alaska, where she traveled by dogsled to villages and fishing camps to immunize the natives of the sub-arctic against tuberculosis. Velma spent time as "Rosie the Riveter" working on liberty ships during World War II. She is proud to be a journeyman boilermaker.

On one occasion in later years when Harry Morrison and Henry Kaiser were touring a shipyard they were considering purchasing, Velma shouted to them to, "Stop the golf cart!" As it skidded to a halt, she jumped off and went to where a welder was cutting. She struck an arc and demonstrated her own skill with the torch, to the delight of the two titans and her fellow boilermaker. "Henry turned to Harry and said, 'What do you have there?' pointing a thumb in my direction. It was good for a couple of rounds of cocktails that night," she laughs.

Then there were the post-World War II days, when she and her family assembled a threshing crew that faced hunger and hardship as it worked the "wild harvest" from

Texas to South Dakota to Idaho and back to California. Later, she became a successful restaurateur while at the same time rearing her three children by herself.

She was thirty-six years old when she met Harry Morrison. Seeing the exuberance with which she lives at eighty-two, it isn't hard to imagine why he must have been enchanted with her "joie de vivre," and understand why he fell in love with her, quickly inviting her into his life. The little farm girl from Tipton, California suddenly found herself drawn onto a world stage.

Beyond her work, I've heard tales of her saving a doomed German Shepherd by donning dark glasses and slipping him into San Francisco's plush St. Francis Hotel under the guise of it being her seeing-eye dog, and another story about her stopping traffic to rescue a turtle from the middle of a busy road on Padre Island in Texas. Her nephew, Frank Windsor, tells a great story about their joint efforts in planning a party. The preparations started with gathering up tables, chairs and party paraphernalia and extended to a stop for cocktails where they watched the scary trucker movie "We Drive by Night." Frank began telling her scary stories. Finally, on the way back to the ranch on dark roads, he pretended the truck engine was sputtering and choking just to hear her squeal and laugh.

An evening visiting with Velma's dear friend Fred Norman brought a host of stories, but many are not included because these are

Velma's memoirs, and the stories came from Fred. He eschewed writing part of Velma's story, and Velma is modest about her own achievements. "But I'm *funny*," she insists, wrinkling her nose. And, she is. Sometimes you just have to be there to appreciate it. Fred still roars at the memories of her playing Sophie Tucker when they were earning money to build the Morrison Center.

As we reviewed the final stages of the book, I told her we needed one more chapter on where she is going from here. "I want to go to heaven," she chirps without hesitation, looking at me as though I've sprouted moss from my head, because where else would she want to go? I have to back up and explain that I meant she is still active and working, so we need to talk about some of the things she still has planned for her life.

At her recent eighty-third birthday party, the announcer told the gathering she was twenty-nine and holding. At that, Velma went forward, grabbed the microphone and, with her eyes sparkling, she promptly let everyone know she was eighty-three and had earned every one of her wrinkles and white hairs. It brought down the house.

An inveterate poker player, Velma often kept the men in stitches at poker games that ran into the wee hours when she and Mr. Morrison were out touring jobsites. One of the men, Johnny Johnson, was her self-appointed guardian, "He wanted to make sure those fellas weren't taking advantage of me. At one point, he went to get drinks for everyone, and while he was gone, I was bidding on the largest pot of the evening. When he got back, he said, 'What have you done?' When the time came to show our cards, I told him I had two pairs, and he said, 'You'll never win with that!' I was kidding him. My two pairs were both pairs of fours, and with four of a kind, I won the whole pot!"

Velma is a one-woman riot. When she says something funny her eyes crinkle into upside-down crescent moons. But Velma never claims any credit for herself in any of the things she says or does. I've enjoyed our frequent visits and conversations tremendously while working furiously to finish her book, knowing all the while that I'll be very sad when it's done.

Velma often talks about her growth over the years. Perhaps in her own eyes, she has grown and changed, but it is hard to imagine she was ever much different than she is today. She is genuine, absolutely authentic. There are no pretenses about her and she puts on no airs. What she thinks is what she says.

Her grandson Drake Shannon tells about attending Germany's *Passion Play* about the life of Christ with his grandmother. During the scene where Christ is being scourged, Velma shouted out from the audience with tears streaming and her voice choked with emotion to "***stop it!***" It pained her so much to watch it that eventually she had to leave the performance. You have to think things would have turned out differently if she had been at the event that inspired the drama. It would have taken more than Pontius Pilate and a few legions of Roman soldiers to deter Velma.

Her faith is monumental. Her generosity and kindness are legendary. Her humor and optimism are always near at hand, and her laughter is infectious. With steadfast faith she has held on through the hardest of times. Even into her eighties, she isn't afraid to tackle anything, or anyone.

In her later years, Velma has lived a life of financial ease, but she continues to use much of her time and treasure in myriad ways that make life better for the people of Idaho, and she has done much to ease the suffering of others. She has loved much and lost much. Her life has not been easy, but she has surely made it memorable.

Yup. It's easy to understand her choice for the title of her book. For Velma Morrison, in triumph and in tragedy, always knew the bluebird would sing tomorrow. Her father, who nicknamed her "Codger," taught her from a tender age that when things seemed darkest, the light from the end of the tunnel would shine to show her the way.

Happy, tragic, funny, frightening, hers has been a rich and textured life. There are few of life's opportunities or challenges that she has not experienced, overcome or embraced. She still lives with great passion.

As a native Californian and a former restaurateur, Velma knows just how to turn life's lemons into lemonade.

*The beggar man and the mighty king are only different in name
for they are treated just the same by fate.*

From the song *Bluebird of Happiness*,
Music by Sandor Harmate. Words by Edward Hayman
Published by Chappell & Co. 1934
Introduced and featured by Jan Pierce in a
Leon Leonidoff production At the Radio City Music Hall

*Everybody put their pants on one
leg at a time.*

Earl Mitchell, Velma's father

The Bluebird Will
Sing Tomorrow

Chapter One

Child of the Great Depression

"Family…family…family," Velma Morrison says, shaking her head and slapping her hand softly on the table to emphasize each repetition of the word. "When you need them, they're always there for you."

Growing up during the Great Depression, Velma learned thrift and simplicity early. Her family worked very hard to have enough, but there was never an abundance. It was not an era when children were indulged as they are today. Her family fared better than many did in those hard economic times, but she saw great suffering and deprivation all around her from an early age, and she was taught to share what she had.

Life hadn't been easy for the Mitchell family. Velma's father, Earl, a thoughtful, handsome man, was the middle child and elder son of an early "baron" who came out from Missouri during the earliest phases of the California Gold Rush. T.J. Mitchell hadn't been a miner. Rather he had furnished supplies for the miners, a merchant who earned a

T.J. Mitchell

Lorraine, Elsie, Harvey, Earl, T.J. Mitchell

tidy sum, which he invested in land and sometimes gambled. Considerably older than his wife, Lorraine, he did the family the disservice of dying when his children were still quite young.

His widow, Lorraine, with her daughter Elsie and son Earl, worked hard to make their farm successful. "Grandmother Mitchell was as tough as she had to be," Velma said. "She

3

kept a shotgun behind the front door, and once the sheriff tried to come and take the pumps from our well because of late payments. Grandmother ran them off with the shotgun. The pumps are still there today."

Earl and Elsie also had another brother, Harvey. Velma said, "Harvey was the original hippie. He didn't stay and work the farm with the rest of the family. Harvey just kind of dis-

Brother and sister Earl and Elsie, in their college graduation picture

appeared and he lived a tough life wandering all over the country, although he'd turn up from time to time in one of our lives, and he always seemed to be happy to see us."

Even in the depths of the Depression no one on their farm ever went hungry, Velma recalls. There might not have been any hard cash, but there was always plenty of food: chickens, turkeys, ducks, various fruit trees, a wealth of fresh vegetables, and a successful dairy whose rich cream was sold to provide the only money the family saw during those hard times.

Velma's mother, Gladys, was a dark-haired beauty of English-Portuguese descent. Gladys was the only daughter of parents who divorced when she was six-years old. Her father left his family behind and went on to train the boxer, Jack Dempsey. After he left the area and remarried, he rarely kept in touch with his daughter. Gladys' mother, Lucy Sarment, also was remarried and Gladys had five half-siblings from that marriage.

"My mother and father met when her family came to work on Grandmother Mitchells' farm. They were both very good looking, and they were immediately attracted to each other, but the marriage was not one that would work out. My mother had a hard time accepting my father and the life of hard work on the farm. I was six-years old when my parents divorced. I also had a three-year old sister, Melva, and an infant brother, Earl.

"After the divorce, my father kept us children on the farm, but my mother stayed in

Gladys

Earl

Gladys, Earl and Velma

close contact with us. She was always there for us. I never had any feeling that I was being neglected, ignored, or that my mother was gone from my life."

Still, it wasn't easy to manage the ranch and take care of the three growing children at the same time. "Baby Earl was placed for a time with my Aunt Laura's Portuguese family." Squealing with laughter, Velma recalls, "They loved that little baby, and he had such good care, but his re-entry into our family wasn't easy. When we picked him up, he could only speak Portuguese. We couldn't understand anything he said.

"Grandmother Mitchell was very firm and terribly old-fashioned. My mother would send us pretty dresses with short sleeves, but Melva and I always had to wear long skirts and long sleeves that made us stand out at school. The other kids often ridiculed us and laughed about our old-fashioned clothing."

As a small child, Velma was never told the specifics of family finances, but times were lean enough that even the smallest child in the household knew the situation was tough. "Cash was scarce, and there were loans to meet, but somehow there was always enough to keep the family going. Once a year Mr. Giannini, the founder of what is now the Bank of America, but at that time was the Bank of Italy, would come to visit all the farmers in the area who had loans with him. He was such a nice gentleman. Grandmother always looked forward to his visits and would make all kinds of preparations. It was just before one of his visits that I first learned about the power of prayer. My family was not a church-going family, but I've since become a Christian.

"Just before Mr. Giannini came to visit, Grandmother had made a luscious date cake because he was very fond of them. It was beautifully frosted with black walnuts sprinkled across the top. I'd gotten into some mischief. I had eaten a lot of the frosting and all of the black walnuts. I still have a sweet tooth! They were so good I didn't even consider the punishment until I had eaten quite a lot of the frosting. And black walnuts are a lot harder to get out of the shells than English walnuts, so I'd not only made a mess of the cake, it would be a lot of work to make more frosting and shell more walnuts to fix it. I was in real trouble when Grandmother came into the dining room and saw what I'd done.

"In those days no one thought about not spanking children when they misbehaved. 'Spare the rod, spoil the child' was Grandmother's motto. She told me after my chore of bringing in the cows we would have a discussion about the cake. Well, I was so afraid, I can tell you, and I prayed the whole time I was getting the cows, 'Please, God…please don't let her whip me.'

"When I got back to the house, Grandmother sat me down and said, 'we've decided what to do with you. You're going to have to pick the nuts out of this entire bucket of walnuts, and you'll have to help me redo the cake.'

"Well, I was surprised and relieved. My first prayer was answered. Otherwise, I'd have gotten a damned good whipping."

There was never a shortage of hard work around the farm, and conditions were primitive. On Saturday nights, the family had a bathtub in the pantry that was filled with water that had to be heated on the stove. Family status determined who got to take the first bath. "We each got our turn, and we all bathed in the same water," Velma chuckles.

The Mitchell Ranch and Gem State Stables in Tipton, California

During the 1930s, the ranch saw a steady influx of immigrants trying to escape from the Dust Bowl. Families from Oklahoma and Texas flooded into the San Joaquin Valley looking for work, food, and a decent place to live. "My Grandmother Mitchell, my father and Aunt Elsie put up tents with board floors to house people. There was no welfare, food stamps or public assistance in those days. It wasn't easy. They did their best to help those poor families. They came to us with not much more than the clothes on their backs. People were destitute, and whole families worked in the fields. I saw it all with my own eyes. I was truly a child of the Depression.

"The members of my family were very generous. Before the Depression, our skim

Velma with her mother Gladys in 1920.

Velma, 18 months old

Velma, one year old

milk was given to the pigs and calves, and we
sold the cream. When people came to us hungry, we shared the food we had, and the skim
milk was given to families. I'm not sure what
they found to feed the animals. When Aunt
Elsie would take the cream to the creamery,
she would take the milk to the people in the
camps. Little kids would run out and greet
her, and she'd pick them up and hug them.
She was a very loving woman. When they

needed shoes or clothes, she'd take them into town and let them pick out whatever things they needed.

"Each camp had about twenty tents. There were two camps on our farm. About thirty families stayed there at any one time. They'd stay with us until they found work.

"During that time, Mr. J. G. Boswell, who came from Georgia, talked Grandmother into growing cotton. We still grow it on the ranch today. Another family had five brothers. Their name was Schott. The brothers came to Grandmother and asked her to let them lease the land and work it. She did.

"One of the men, who was born and raised on the farm, still works our ranch. He is now in his 60s, a very successful farmer, working thousands of acres. All of his family members now own their own, huge farms too, and he's a very wealthy man in his own right.

"My father, Earl, was a good and kind man, and a philosopher. Both he and Aunt Elsie went to Stockton and were college graduates although, in retrospect, it isn't easy to think what his degree might have been in," Velma said. She is quite certain, however, it wasn't in business. "He was kind of a hard luck guy. He started all kinds of things that didn't work out. He tried anything and everything to make a living. Once he decided to make bootleg whiskey during Prohibition. I can still remember when the sheriff came to the farm and hauled him away. I was small so it was very frightening, and it was a terrible embarrassment to my mother.

Grandmother Mitchell with Velma around 1923

"Another time, after my parents were divorced, my father and I moved to Rialto and I was helping him. He started a dairy delivery service. Daddy said to me: 'Codger, I am going to call it the Exclusive Dairy Service, because the milk we deliver is from hybrid Jersey cows and it has an exceptionally high cream content.' It was a good idea, but we were caught in a milk war where milk went down to six cents a quart. There was no way the service could survive on that, so back to the farm we went."

15

Lorraine, Elsie, Earl, and Harvey Mitchell on a trip to Mexico

To his young daughter, Earl was still a hero. "He was very philosophical and when we'd go around to places, he would talk to me about life. He used to say things to me like, 'only you can tell whether something is right or wrong, Codger. Your conscience will tell you.' Despite the many hard times he went through, he still maintained an upbeat attitude toward life, telling me 'when you have dark days, the light on the other end of the tunnel will see you through.'"

Earl's optimism was absorbed into every fiber of young Velma's character. It's a trait that has served her well through the years, giving her the strength to carry on through the hardest times of her life.

Chapter Two

The Greatest Joys

"There were no ultrasound tests in those days. But if there had been, I wouldn't have needed one. From the first stirrings of life, I knew my baby was going to be a girl," Velma says with a soft laugh. "And when Judith was born in May 1939, she was strong and healthy. She had the right number of fingers and toes, and the biggest, most beautiful brown eyes I'd ever seen. She was a darling little baby girl. I was delighted."

Life was perfect. Velma Vivian Mitchell Gatewood was still a teenager, and she had everything she wanted in life.

Roland Gatewood was ten years her senior, and he had been married previously, but she was young enough that she didn't wonder why his first marriage hadn't worked. She loved him, and his past didn't matter. She was still in high school when they met. Roland had a flashy sports car in a day when that meant everything. He was handsome and she was swept off her feet. They went dancing and night clubbing, and she was ecstatic to be accepted by him and to be in his company.

Judith Vivian Gatewood in San Francisco

"One night we went with friends to Las Vegas and were married. Through my uncle I got a job working for the phone company. I went to work and learned to be a telephone operator back in the days when all calls were handled by central operators and we had to manually connect the caller with the party they wanted to reach. 'Number, please?' I'd ask each time the line rang. Every day I drove the sixty miles from Taft to Bakersfield, but

Judy and Velma in Richmond, California. 1944

the distance didn't matter. I was making good money and we were happily married."

When she found out she was pregnant, Velma was ecstatic. "I quit work and started staying at home. My mother and grandmother came to visit me. We dinged around and spent lots of time making tiny clothes for the new baby. They were all pink. Nothing but pink. First I'd picked out the name Linda because it was popular at the time, but then I discovered the name Judith in the Bible and thought it was lovely. Judith Vivian. My mother's middle name was Vivian, and so is mine."

Posed with a question about what the greatest joys of her life have been, Velma's eyes grow soft and misty, but her answer comes without a moment of hesitation: "Oh, holding my babies. There's nothing like holding a new life in your arms."

The birth of her daughter changed Velma profoundly. A young wife and mother, she was delighted with her new daughter and her new role, but her happiness proved fleeting when she began to realize that Roland was a womanizer.

The final straw came the day her mother told her, "'When you were in the hospital having the baby, he was with another woman.' It was a horrible shock to me, one I held against my mother for many years. But, of course, it wasn't her fault.

"I was heartbroken. When Judith was a month old I left Roland and moved back to

Five generations: Velma, Judith with Alec in arms,
Gladys, and Grandma Lucy

Tipton to live with my father and grandmother on the farm.

"For a while, I worked as a soda jerk and
Aunt Ethel Sarment took care of baby Judith
while I worked. But I eventually decided I
needed to try once more, to give my husband
another chance. I desperately wanted the three
of us to be a family. I took Judith and we
boarded the bus in Tulare and rode the one
hundred fifty miles back to Taft to make
amends with Roland."

Deep in thought, Velma was far, far away
as the bus traveled along the highway and she
stared out the window with her infant daugh-

21

ter on her lap. "I still loved my husband and was determined to put aside my hurt feelings and patch things up for the sake of Judith. She was so tiny, and I thought she should have her father."

Arriving back at their house, she waited on the porch until he arrived home at 11 p.m. "I want to patch things up. We can make our marriage work," Velma declared simply. His reply seared her soul, and the hurt carries down through the years. "Aah, you just wanted some good loving," he sneered as he bounded up the steps and opened the front door. She and Judith spent the night sleeping in the extra bedroom and he put them back on the bus the next morning.

"You always have a soft spot for your first love," she says quietly more than six decades later, "but we met once again, later on down the road, and that time he cured my feelings for him forever."

Still in her teens and facing the fact that her marriage was over, Velma returned to Bakersfield and began nurse's training. Her Aunt Ethel in Tulare adored baby Judith. She cared for the baby and gave her lots of love and attention while Velma went back to nursing school.

During one term, Velma had an opportunity to go to Alaska as part of the program. Her mother and Grandma Lucy drove her to Seattle, and in the tense days just prior to World War II, she started the long journey to Nome for some practical experience with the

Velma polishing her Ford during the shipyard days.

Public Health Service. When the ship stopped briefly at Dutch Harbor to take on fresh water, no one was allowed to set foot ashore. Velma, however, spotted a friend from school who had been among the first to join the Army as they saw a war approaching. The young soldier was walking guard duty on the docks. Velma called out to him. "Gil! Gil Galliducci! Hi, Gil! It's me...Velma!" Surprised to see an old school friend, he responded enthusiastically to her call and helped her figure a way to get off the ship for a short visit.

Landing in Nome was no easy task. Alaska's admission to statehood was more than twenty years in the future, and it would be nearly fifty years before a causeway was built to get freight into Nome. It was still very much the "Last Frontier." The shallow Bering Sea demanded that ocean vessels lighter their loads onto barges to make their way to the docks. The young student nurses were thrilled by the adventure of the trip, but stunned by housing with "honeybuckets" instead of sewers, water that was delivered by trucks once a week, and the primitive hospital facilities the town afforded.

Although it was May and "break-up" had washed the winter's ice out to sea, the tundra held fast to its mantle of snow. Mud continued to be knee-deep in the streets for nearly another month. Boardwalks rose above the mud along Front Street, but they were sparingly used throughout the tiny treeless town, surrounded by tundra and clinging to the edge of the coast as though from force of habit.

Reaching the far-flung camps and villages of Northwest Alaska was not an easy matter either. Wrapped snugly in furs and blankets, the young nurses settled into baskets on the dogsleds as mushers drove their teams over the snow and still-frozen rivers to the villages and fishing camps around Norton Sound. She went as far as Unalakleet, ninety miles away on the south end of the sound, immunizing the native population that still had little defense against the tuberculosis carried by the white prospectors and settlers pushing into the territory. As the summer wore on and the snow finally yielded, the nurses went on flights aboard tiny planes outfitted with pontoons for water landings near various camps and villages.

The Eskimo children were beautiful babies with sturdy, compact limbs, warm brown complexions and huge dark eyes that watched solemnly as Velma prepared their injections. Once inoculated, they voiced their hearty objections. She'd snuggle the children, but that made her all the more lonely for Judith, thousands of miles away, across the vast waters they'd been told were bristling with Japanese submarines.

Returning home, Velma's mother and Grandma Lucy picked Velma up in Seattle and drove her back to Bakersfield. She sat in the back seat on the way to California, and she snuggled her baby close. What a joyous reunion it was with Judith!

It was Velma's first Alaskan experience, but it was far from being her last. Little could the young student nurse have imagined that one day she'd return to Alaska as the wife of an engineer who would spearhead the construction of the Alaskan Pipeline that would bring untold oil wealth to the inhabitants of the isolated Great Land by the 1970s.

Shortly after her return home, Velma went to church with friends on a beautiful Sunday morning in early December. Leaving the services, they were stunned by the news that Pearl Harbor had been bombed. On December 7, 1941, war was no longer a matter of speculation. Hearing the news, one of her friends who already was in the military and was home on furlough grumbled, "I knew nothing good would come out of going to church."

As the country was hurled from the last throes of the Great Depression into another world war, Velma's mother remarried. She and her new husband, Tom Neff, were going to work in the shipyards in Richmond, California. Suddenly there were marvelous opportunities opening in the manufacturing industries, where there weren't nearly enough workers to fill the heavy demand for ships and munitions.

Velma and Anita Woods were already old friends from their school days. Anita was tiny, with shining black hair, petite and pretty, with a youthful energy that matched Velma's own.

They'd gone to school together in Bakersfield, and they were eager to move where things were starting to happen. "My mother and Tom had heard that you could make great money working in the shipyards in Richmond. The four of us went up there together. We lived in a tent out in a field for a while because there were no places to stay. Housing was difficult to find. Everyone was working on ships. Finally the four of us got an apartment together for a while until Mother and Tom were able to get a place of their own.

Walking into a little shed that served as the personnel office, Velma was hired on the spot as a first-aid nurse, even though she had not yet completed the nursing program. Anita went to work as a secretary in the business office. They shared an apartment to save expenses and spent their evenings going to dances and nightclubs.

One day Velma was patching a cut one of the workers had sustained on the job. "What do you do?" she asked. The woman said she was a welder. Velma was curious and responded. "How much do you make for doing a job like that?"

The young welder was making substantially more than Velma. "How do you get a job like that?" she asked. The woman told her she had to join the boilermakers' union. "It would be well worth it. You sure earn a helluva lot more than I do!"

Velma and Anita went in promptly the next morning and signed up for the boilermakers' union. They learned to weld and cut with a torch. Wearing huge aprons, leather pants and hoods, they learned how to strike an arc and began working on the mighty liberty ships.

Velma went to several schools to become a journeyman burner working with the shipfitters who built the metal structure of the huge ships. She preferred that job because they could wear jeans instead of the heavy leather pants, and they just had to wear little goggles instead of the cumbersome hoods. The company asked for volunteers to go up high on the ship and work. Velma was a journeyman burner when she volunteered to go up on the high decks. She thought it was a good idea because she'd be able to make much more money. She reported for work and the shipfitter said, "oh, God no…what do we have here?" She discovered that she was the

Ron and Velma Shannon on their wedding day.

first woman to report for work up on the high decks.

Velma was up there on her own, although she had a laborer to drag the hoses. She was doing a good job. She cut the templates for the stacks of the liberty ships with accuracy and

Ron and Velma's wedding

speed, and she was proud of her journeyman boilermaker's status.

The pieces she was cutting out were held in place by little welded "dogs" so they wouldn't drop onto the deck below. The burner could safely kneel on the huge circle with-

Ron and Velma
Shannon in
Messina, New
York

out having to move hoses and gas containers
all over the area. One day, however, the little
dogs gave way beneath her. The plate she had
been cutting crashed three stories below her,
and Velma was left hanging through the hole.
She managed to hang on with her elbows
akimbo over the edges, screaming for help. "It
seemed like forever until I was pulled out of
the hole and back to safety."

She decided even the best money being
paid wasn't worth the risk of her life, so she
told her boss, "I'm not going up on the high
decks anymore." She was given a job on the
ground, burning the same kind of little dogs
that had given way beneath her. She kept her

eyes open and eventually found a great job as a "ship to shore" operator, passing calls along as the liberty ships put out to sea on their trial runs. It paid well, allowed her to have her weekends off, and didn't involve working in high places.

"The operator's job was a good one, which I really loved. There were lots of handsome, young sailors who would come through where I worked. 'We're shipping out tomorrow night. How about a date?' they'd ask. Oh, they were handsome! We'd go dancing, and night clubbing. We had a lot of fun with them," Velma says.

During the time Velma was working in the shipyards, she again fell in love. Ronald Chester Shannon was a supervisor, deferred from the draft for his essential work. He was a supervisor charged with building the ships that were so desperately needed for the war effort.

After dating for some time, she and Ronald went to Reno and tied the knot. She continued to work, and they were able to bring Judith up to live with them. Now a first-grader, Judith was enrolled at the Immaculate Conception School in San Francisco, a boarding school. "It was just great. I could pick her up whenever I wasn't working, and Judy spent weekends with us. It was a happy time."

Finally, the war was over, and the couple awaited the birth of a new addition to their family. On September 4, 1946, their first son,

Ron, was born. In the post-war days, hospitals were jammed with deliveries of new arrivals. Velma had to go through labor in the hallway of the hospital. It was lined with beds of expectant mothers in various phases of labor. Men weren't allowed into the delivery room in those days, but Velma's husband stood by her side throughout the labor. "Just before the baby arrived I had a terrible pain and let out a scream. The janitor was standing nearby, sweeping the hall. He was terrified when I screamed and he disappeared down the hall, leaving his broom where he had stood. We had to laugh.

"Ronnie was a beautiful baby. His dad was thrilled to have a son, and I was happy to see he was healthy and robust. It was wonderful to have a new baby."

Her mother and sister Melva took the train from Tulare to come and see baby Ronnie. Although Ron and Velma's marriage already had many problems and her life was not always easy, her growing family made Velma very happy.

During that time, Roland showed back up in her life after his discharge. While he had not been much of a husband, he'd always paid child support for Judith and he cared deeply about his daughter. Eventually he had been drafted and he was in England throughout the war. Even while he was in the service, he made arrangements for her to receive regular child support.

"Then one day we received a letter from him. He was coming home on a troop ship, and he wanted very much to see his little daughter. Even though I was married to Ron at the time, I still got a little heartthrob when I'd think about seeing him again. I wondered if my legs would hold me up and how I could even get them to move. He was my first love, and I was still holding onto something that once was there.

"We made arrangements to meet for dinner at the Hotel Fresno. We set the date and time, and I told him I'd bring Judy to see her father. She was a beautiful, bouncy little girl. She had no memory of him, but she smiled at him and she was pleased and friendly when he hugged her.

"It was a far different experience for me, however. As I stood there and looked at him, I wondered how I ever could have spent all that time holding onto memories, loving this guy and feeling bad about what I'd lost. We had dinner and he left. That was the end. I kept wondering how he could be like that. He was not at all as he had appeared to my teenage eyes. He wasn't any different than he had been, but I was different. I stood there looking at him that day, and I finally realized what a big mistake I had made.

"I had grown up during the years since our divorce."

Chapter Three

The Wild Harvest

Grandmother Mitchell had died before the war, leaving Velma's father Earl and his sister Elsie to run the family's farm with help from the tenants living there. Because of the war's insatiable appetite for labor, they still were running it more or less on their own.

"Then with the end of the war, work at the shipyards ended. My father came to visit us and he suggested the family do the 'wild harvest.' That's what they call it when a harvesting crew takes big trucks and harvesters from state to state, finding jobs harvesting grain, and then moving on again to the next farm," Velma said. "It's a job that sounds romantic to the uninitiated. It involves traveling around the country, testing your ability to adapt and survive. The truth falls closer to its being darned hard work with tremendous overhead and an uncertain future."

With the family's new plans taking shape, Velma's father arranged workers to help on the farm so he could go on the road and do the wild harvest. Perhaps the fact that her

Velma, Ronnie, and Penny the dog. No more trailers.

father had suggested the venture should have
tipped them off, but the family was ready for
the adventure and the promise of huge returns
on their investment.

Velma and Ron sold their house in
Richmond. "It was the first thing we bought
when we could afford it. It cost something like
three thousand dollars, and it was really cute,
but we sold the house and bought a trailer.
"Sometimes even now my kids suggest we get
a travel trailer and go around the country. Not
me! I had enough of trailers back then."

The family, at that point, in addition to
Velma and Ron, included Gladys and her husband Tom, her father Earl and his wife Ruby,
her sister Melva and her husband Archie.

"Wasn't it awkward for your mother and father, now long divorced and both remarried, to be partners in the wild harvest venture? " I asked.

"Not really," Velma answered. "Time had mellowed them. The two couples had a great time together. The four of them often stayed up late and played cards, laughing and joking. And all of us had something very important in common: all of us had mortgaged everything we owned.

"Off we went to Amarillo on our first trip, a long line of red harvesters and trailers. Each family had two harvesters except Mom and Tom, who had one. We were a sorry-looking bunch. When we got to Texas, we were a little bit ahead of the harvest. Melva and I went out and found our first job. We set up camp the next morning. Melva and I each had two children. Mom and Tom watched the kids while we went out and arranged work for our crew. The first farmer we talked with was just testing his wheat for water and sugar content when we got there. It was about a week until we could start harvesting, but he hired us. We were excited and went out arranging other jobs for the crew.

"The night before we were going to start harvesting, the farmer where we were staying came out shouting for all of us to get into the cellar. 'Don't you see that funnel cloud coming?' he shouted to us. A tornado was on its way, but none of us knew what that meant. We had never seen such a thing before. He herded all of us into the shelter. We just barely were safely down there before all hell broke loose over our heads. It seemed like forever that things crashed and pounded above the cellar.

"When the twister had passed, and we emerged from beneath the ground, everything we had was in shambles. Everything was damaged. The camp tents were knocked down, everything was banged up, and lots of things were missing. It was a mess! We had to set up all over again.

"When we finally got started on the harvest, things began to go a little better. Big hailstones from the tornado had ruined many of the crops in the area, but fortunately, there was no crop damage to the farms where we had arranged to work."

With four or five hired men, the family began moving along. Finishing in Texas, they began to thread their way north as the crops matured. They were off to Oklahoma, Kansas, Nebraska and South Dakota.

Times were still hard. Everyone pitched in and worked from morning until night. Their expenses were eating up everything they were earning. When they arrived in Colorado they were dismayed to find that a hailstorm had gone through shortly before their arrival, and much of the wheat crop in the region was destroyed. They were working hard and still it was nearly impossible to keep the family and harvesting crew adequately fed.

Finally they found a big job in Winner, South Dakota. But they had to wait for the grain to dry. It was hard, hungry times. "One Sunday after church, the family we were working for invited us to their home for Sunday dinner. We fixed dinner for the hired men and went to join them. Sometimes it surprises you to realize how kind, caring and generous people are. They were facing hard times too, but they were still willing to share with us.

"It was a beautiful spread. There were plates filled with all sorts of good foods: fried chicken, potatoes and gravy, and fresh vegetables. We were hungry, and it was more than just good food to us. It was a feast.

"As I was serving up two-year old Ronnie's plate, he looked woefully at the chicken livers I had put there and he refused to eat them. 'No, mama, no! That's ca-ca.' It seems funny now, but his childish innocence sure embarrassed us at the time!

"About that same time, Ronnie broke himself of having a bottle. One day he was standing on the truck seat next to me. He was just darling. He was wearing tiny overalls and he had the cutest little hat. When he finished his bottle, he threw it out the open window, and it was gone. He cried all that night, but I told him if he threw it out, it was gone. He never used a bottle again."

The family moved on, following the harvest. Velma and Melva worked hard to sell the threshing services. They had good workers on their crew, and they had great success in finding jobs as they went along, but often they had to wait for the grain to ripen. Delays did not fill the family's coffers, and the long days and weeks of waiting didn't stop everyone from getting hungry.

One day Velma and Melva were on their way into town to check the mail. They were on a dirt road in South Dakota, and suddenly they spotted something peculiar on the road ahead of them. It was as though a blanket was being shaken over the road. As they neared, they could see it was a huge flock with probably a hundred chickens flapping and squabbling, enjoying a royal feast that some passing grain truck had spilled in the middle of the road.

Melva looked at her sister with a twinkle. "Do you see what I see?"

"I see tonight's dinner!" Velma laughed, gunning the engine. Ten chickens were down when they looked back over their shoulders. Instantly, the sisters looked at each other again, and agreed without a word. They turned the car around and went back for a second helping of chickens. "Everyone ate well that night," Velma chuckles.

Unfortunately, chickens didn't fall like manna from heaven every day. Sometimes, however, the men were able to hunt pheasants while they waited for jobs. Once they were so broke they had to wire home to a friend who sent them a thousand dollars to help tide the crew along. Somehow they managed. Velma muses, "After all these years it's still hard to remember how we managed, but somehow, with God's help, we did."

When work was winding up in South Dakota, it was on to Montana and then into Idaho where Velma was introduced to the Gem State. "We were broke once again, waiting for the harvest, trying to keep the entire family and all five hired men fed. It was a constant struggle."

The first stop in Idaho was Malad City. By this time they were desperate for groceries and supplies. It fell to Velma and Melva to find a way to feed the crew. They went into town and looked into the window at the grocery store. "No point in putting it off," Velma thought. She stepped up and grabbed the handle, swinging open the creaking door. "What are you going to use to pay for supplies, your good looks?" Melva inquired.

"Something like that. Don't you think I have an honest face?" Velma responded. Stepping up to the counter, she asked to speak to the owner.

"You already are," he answered, eyeing her steadily.

Identifying herself and her sister, Velma went on to explain about their situation and told him where they had been hired. She looked the grocer straight in the eye. "The harvest won't be ready to start until next week and we're very low on funds. We're broke, in fact, and we need groceries for our crew.

Could we sign a tab for the supplies and pay you when we're finished?"

The grocer looked directly at her. He reached his hand across the counter to shake hers. "You girls go and pick out whatever you need. You can sign a tab for it." It was Velma's first experience with Idaho and Idahoans. His kindly response that day planted in her heart and mind the first seeds of her deep love for the place and its people.

Chuckling with satisfaction at the dusty memory, Velma adds, "and we paid him back, too. Every cent of it."

From Malad City, they were on to Soda Springs, and then they worked on through Utah, Oregon and home to California. When they returned to the farm at Tipton, they held a family council and the verdict was instant and unanimous: there had to be a better way to make a living. The equipment was sold. There'd be no more trailers in Velma's life.

"Sometimes today my kids will say we should get a travel trailer and see the country. Not me," Velma insists. "I'll never travel around like that again!"

Ronnie's second birthday was on the road during the
wild harvest days.

Chapter Four

As God is my Witness...

One of Velma's shining teenage memories was when she and Anita met and shook the hand of Clark Gable, the king of Hollywood, as his limousine pulled through the gate where he was making an appearance at a fiesta at the Kern County Park. "I didn't wash my hand for a week," she giggles. In spite of the many acquaintances and friends she's made over the years, and her own prominence, the memory of meeting Gable remains a moment of undiminished luster.

All right...it was quite a stretch to work Clark Gable into the story, but Velma cherishes that moment and wanted it included in her memoirs. And, it was not Velma, but rather Scarlet O'Hara in *Gone with the Wind*, who vowed, "As God is my witness, I shall never be hungry again." Perhaps it was the result of the long, hungry summer working the wild harvest that Melva and Velma decided on going into the restaurant business.

After the family sold the trailers and the long red line of harvesting equipment, it was time to face the Big Question: "What do we do now?"

Velma was pregnant with Gary, her second son, soon after the time they were working the harvest. Gary Allan Shannon was born on Oct. 26, 1950.

Gary's birth was a thrill. "Holding my baby in my arms was the greatest thrill of my life," Velma often says. "Gary was such a darling little baby, and a handsome, loving young boy. We were thrilled to have another son."

Shortly after Gary was born, Melva discovered a restaurant that was for sale in Corcoran, only twelve miles from the Mitchell farm. The sisters had plenty of experience cooking for their families and the harvesting crews. But a restaurant, they wondered?

"Do you think you want to tackle something like this?" Melva asked.

"What do we know about running a restaurant?" Velma replied. "In fact, what do we know about being in business at all?" Nonetheless, they purchased it. The Home Town Café was across the street from the J. G. Boswell Company, which then owned, and still does own, the largest irrigated farms in the world with locations in California, Arizona, and Australia.

Boswell's workers, supervisors and visitors from around the world kept the café hopping. After the desperate times on the road, the sisters were concerned that they might not have enough money for a down payment and still be able to make the monthly payments on the place. Lawrence Ellison, the old friend who had sent them money when they were stranded on the road, stepped in once again and co-signed for a loan. Undeterred by their lack of business knowledge, it was theirs, and they were in business.

"Farmers go to work early," Velma recalls. "I had to be there every morning at four o'clock to make the coffee. Fortunately we were able to keep the cook, who had been there for a long time. Our specialty was a hearty breakfast."

For the next three years, Velma and Melva worked long days, six days a week. They made a lot of friends and they immensely enjoyed the work. Best of all, they were always able to keep up with their payments.

The café kept Melva and Velma busy while Bill Kinsella was hanging onto the Mitchell farm.

— — — — — — —

"After Grandmother died, my father and Aunt Elsie inherited the farm. Elsie had Grandmother's business sense, her sense of purpose and her boundless energy. Despite the hard work and short supplies of those days, Elsie had a tendency toward weight. Later, when she married, the family was somewhat surprised at her choice. She married Bill Kinsella.

"Bill Kinsella was what could be called a gentleman farmer if you were being kind, or a very lazy man if you weren't. He was an Englishman who was very tall, medium build with light brown, thinning hair and he put on a lot of airs. He dressed in an English style, and he was not a man who was naturally disposed to the kind of hard work it took to keep the farm afloat.

"Aunt Elsie was not a classic beauty, but she was a lovely, gentle woman. She was very tall and stately, with dark blonde hair. My sister and I loved her dearly. Like Grandmother Mitchell, she had worked very hard on the farm. During the Great Depression, when we would visit the people migrating through our area looking for work, she was well known for her generosity. Everyone loved her.

"Elsie and my father kept things together. They fixed what was broken, and they did the day-to-day work of running things. When we went to do the wild harvest, Elsie hired extra help to keep things going. It wasn't Bill who worked the ranch." Velma tries to recall exactly what Bill did do to fill his days. The search bears no fruit. There are no clear answers, no memories of him actually doing any kind of real work.

"Some time after Elsie and Bill were married, Bill's niece Patty moved from England with two small children and also took up residence at the ranch. She didn't show much inclination toward working either, so she did not get along well with my Aunt Elsie. Eventually Patty and her children moved into town. Shortly afterward, Bill followed.

"He sued Elsie for divorce. And, as if breaking her heart wasn't enough, he also demanded alimony. In response to his claim that it had been his hard work that kept the farm going, a judge granted him the alimony, something that was unheard of in those days. Uncomplainingly, the hardworking Elsie assumed yet another burden.

"A couple of years after the divorce, Elsie received a call from Patty late one night. There had been trouble between her and Uncle Bill. She begged Elsie to come into town and help them sort things out. Elsie jumped into her truck and headed for town.

"On her way into town, at a sharp bend in the road noted for ugly crashes, Elsie's truck was hit and demolished. Badly hurt in the crash, Elsie was taken to the nearest hospital. She lingered for several days, but we were there when the horrible verdict was issued. One leg was crushed so badly in the crash that it couldn't be saved. 'I don't think I'll live through this operation, girls,' she told us as we sat tearfully begging her to hang on and have hope."

That night Bill Kinsella arrived to say good-bye to his former wife. Somehow, during that meeting, he managed to have her sign papers turning the farm over to him for the rest of his life. Velma and Melva were aghast. The Mitchell's farm was falling into the greedy hands of Bill Kinsella? It was unthinkable to them, especially after the way he had treated Elsie. They asked her how she could do that, and she said to them, "it was only given to me to use while I was here. After Bill is gone, it goes back to all of you."

Sadly, Elsie was correct about not living through the surgery.

Coping with the loss of their beloved aunt, the girls and their brother Earl also were faced with the fact that Bill Kinsella now had possession of their family farm. Wherever they had wandered over the years, the Mitchell farm had always been the center of their lives, the place that stood as "home" in their hearts.

As the years went by, not surprisingly, Bill didn't pay the taxes on the farm, and he let it go into default. Faced with the ultimate loss of their inheritance, Velma, Melva and their brother Earl hired an attorney. Lawrence Ellison, who took over receivership of the farm, was able to help them convince the authorities that the taxes would be paid.

The Mitchell siblings mortgaged everything they owned once again to recover ownership of the property. The courts awarded them title to the property but upheld Bill's rights to use of the property for his life expectancy. Velma, her brother and sister, had to compensate Bill for the value of using the land for what could be presumed to be the rest of his life based on insurance actuarial tables. They grumbled with the decision, but they complied.

Under Mr. Ellison's able care, the land was once again leased to knowledgeable farmers who were able to work it and pay off the mortgage within a few years.

Several years after Elsie died, Velma's father was driving along the same stretch of road where his sister had been hit, when his car was hit by a drunk driver. Earl died shortly thereafter, in the same room of the same hospital where Elsie died just a few years earlier. He was fifty-nine years old.

Despite the urging of his children, Earl had refused to marry until they were grown and on their own. He and Ruby had been married only seven years at the time of his death.

When he died, Earl left each of his children a little money. He had always wanted to go to Peru, so Velma, Melva and their brother Earl decided to take a trip to South America in his memory. They decided on Caracas, Venezuela, because they had friends near there. They secured passports, made the arrangements and were ready to go when their plans changed. Earl couldn't go. Nonetheless, the sisters decided to go ahead with the trip.

Their friends formerly had lived near the family farm in Tipton, but moved to Venezuela several years earlier. They planned to visit the neighbors, but wanted to spend some time in other places before visiting their friends who lived in the interior of the country. Velma and Melva booked rooms in a lovely hotel in Caracas. When they checked in, they realized their money wouldn't last long if they stayed at the hotel. Although they didn't read Spanish, Velma's Spanish/English dictionary helped them to search the papers and they located a pleasant rooming house where they could afford to stay for a while longer.

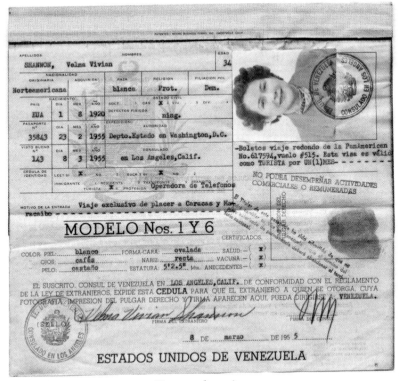

Venezuelan visa

They scheduled a bus trip to the interior to visit their friends, but as they were boarding, Velma grabbed Melva and pulled her back as she realized there were no other women on the bus. They waited. Eventually another bus came along that had other women passengers, so they felt safer traveling on it.

The buses were old hulking things driven by "Flying Tigers" who whipped them around narrow, winding mountain roads. Although they didn't know much Spanish, Velma checked her dictionary and quickly learned the word "despaso" for "slowly!" which she frequently shouted out from her seat.

They often went out dancing. One evening, a very handsome man begged Melva to marry him and take him back to North America. He didn't seem concerned that she already was married. The women told him they weren't interested in providing him with a green card. However, they did want to entertain their friends. One evening they were able to talk Mrs. Bermudas, their landlady, into allowing them to cook dinner for some of their dancing partners.

Shopping in another language wasn't easy. Velma forgot her dictionary when they went to the market, and neither of them knew the word for chicken. There was no one nearby who was able to translate for them. Velma conquered the language barrier by flapping her arms, throwing her head in the air and crowing, "cock-a-doodle-doo." The butcher nodded and said "pollo." With that, he smiled and produced a chicken for their approval. "The fellas all came for the dinner and we had a great time," Velma recalls with a laugh.

The other highlight of that trip was that all the women admired the sisters' clothing. Eventually they decided to sell their pretty dresses. When their return flight landed in New York, they went out and bought all new clothing. "It was better than Christmas," Velma laughs.

Gary was about four years old when his father left to find work on construction jobs. It

Ronnie, Velma, and Gary when Velma and Melva had their restaurant in Corcoran.

was an unofficial separation for the Shannons, as things hadn't gone well between them for some time, and they parted with no intention of getting back together.

Velma and Melva had owned the restaurant for three years when they decided to sell it. Velma moved to Bakersfield with her children and found a small house to rent. Melva and her family also moved to Bakersfield about the same time, but Melva decided to start a lumber company with their brother, Earl.

For the first time in her life, Velma was truly on her own. Judy was in high school, Ron was in fourth grade and Gary was starting first grade. She found a job working the night shift from 11 p.m. until 7 a.m. as a waitress at an all-night truck stop. "It wasn't easy, but that way I could come home from work in the morning, wake up the kids and get them breakfast. Then I saw them off to school. I slept while they were at school, cooked them dinner and spent the evenings with them. When I got them all tucked in bed, I was off to work for the night.

"It was a hard life, but it gave me an opportunity to learn more about the restaurant business. This was a big all-night truck stop, not like the little cafe Melva and I had."

A few years later, when Judy was still in high school, Velma was again thinking about her own business. As she was considering that possibility, her husband Ron came back and told her he wanted to start over, to give their marriage another chance. He was working in Messina, New York, for a company called Morrison-Knudsen, and he urged her to pack up the family and move back there with him. For the children's sake, Velma agreed to give their marriage another try.

Judy wanted to stay in California, so she coaxed her mother to allow her to stay with

Gladys and Tom. Velma conceded reluctantly. Agonized to be leaving her daughter behind, Velma and the boys drove across the country. It took many days in their old Chrysler, in the time before the construction of the Interstate that helped to speed travelers on their way.

Ron had found a nice place for the family, and many of the friends he was working with were people Velma knew from the shipyards. The boys loved the area and the house. She gave it a try, but nothing was working for the pair. "We just weren't right for each other. I was a nervous wreck," she said, "and eventually I broke out with shingles. I hated the place. Messina seemed as though it was always overcast, cold and wet, and I was used to making my own decisions."

The day after Thanksgiving, she told Ron she had to go home to California. He had tried. She had tried. They just couldn't make it happen. "It just wasn't there," she recalls. "I'd never have forgiven myself if we hadn't tried, but we finally knew for certain that the marriage was over."

Packed up and on the road once again, it took four long days and nights of driving for Velma and the two boys to get back to Bakersfield. They slept in the car one night, and stayed in motels on the alternate night, so they could take showers and get cleaned up. As the drive took them away from Messina and nearer to California, Velma's spirits lifted, and she knew everything would be fine. "I was so happy when I drove into my mother's place and saw Judy!"

Chapter Five

The Broiler

Velma still liked the idea of starting her own business, but before she made the final decision, she went to her minister and asked him to pray with her. "I had great faith, but as a single mother with three children, I had to know it was the right thing to do. As we prayed, I began to feel the idea take hold. I'm a strong person, but I had to know it was the right thing to do. You have to have faith. You can't do it on your own."

With a loan from a friend, Velma finally started her restaurant, building it from the ground up with her own ideas. "It was great fun driving to Los Angeles, picking out what I needed and doing the planning.

"The Broiler was beautifully decorated, and it could seat more than a hundred people. It had silver curtains, and an overall pink-and-gray color scheme. We served breakfast, lunch and dinner seven days a week.

"I was very strict with my girls. Every morning I'd hold an inspection. Their uniforms were pink and gray striped and they

The Broiler in Bakersfield

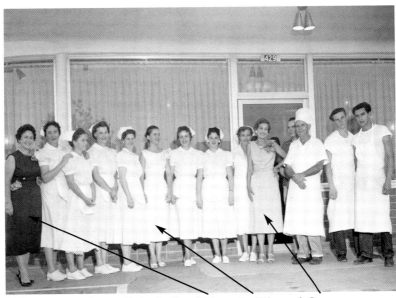

The Broiler staff, including Velma, Judith, and Cora Leadbetter.

The restaurant could seat one hundred.

wore starched white aprons and little hats.
Their white shoes had to be neatly polished.

"We had an honor roll where everyone
would sign whenever they broke dishes. I was
on it too, and I broke more than anyone else.
One time I dropped an entire tray of glasses
with a huge crash."

Although she'd had to go heavily into
debt to get it going, the restaurant was an
instant, resounding success. Customers
packed into the huge rooms. Everything was
made from scratch: salad dressings, jams and
jellies, breads, rolls, pastries, Danish, bread
pudding and all sorts of fabulous desserts.

Patrons wanting seating often had to wait patiently in lines on the sidewalk outside the building.

The Broiler was directly across from the courthouse in Bakersfield. To cater to its clientele, she opened a back room called the Bailiff Room where juries were brought in for their meals. There was no talking with those guests. No visiting, or any kind of contact, was allowed. Only one waitress was allowed to serve them.

The Broiler didn't accept reservations, although it had many regular customers. "One was Judge Jillitch. Recently widowed, the judge ate at the restaurant three times a day. In what might have been a substitute for being at home, he always sat in the same spot. The judge would uncomplainingly eat whatever was brought to him, but he wouldn't allow menus to be presented. He wanted his newspaper set next to his place in the morning, and *Time* magazine had to be there at other meals.

"It's a strange experience to work with the public," Velma said. "Especially in restaurants. If you think artists are temperamental, you should see how chefs behave!

"We had a chef for steaks and chops, a pastry chef, another for salads and still another for sandwiches. Our kitchen was open, and it was beautiful, all stainless steel, and it was scrubbed down every night.

"It was always as busy as could be. One day I walked through the kitchen and the meat chef said, 'Who went through my kitchen?' I told him I had. He said, 'I don't let anyone go through my kitchen while I'm working.' I told him I was the proprietor and I could go through if I wanted.

"With that, his chef's hat came off and he was out the door. There were orders hanging all over the rack, and I wondered how I would fill them. If it hadn't been for Ernie, the salad chef, I don't know what I'd have done. I did not know how to make a steak medium rare or medium well done.

"While I was trying to figure out what to do, Ernie came over and said, 'If I take over Harold's job, how much more would I make?' He was satisfied with my answer, so he stepped in and did it. Ernie did a wonderful job. He was still there when I sold the place several years later."

Despite the grind of working long, hard days, Velma recalls those years as "happy, happy times." The restaurant had proven to be hugely successful. She was able to hire a woman who helped to take care of the children when she was working. Each Sunday the family ate breakfast at The Broiler, went to church and then headed off to her sons' favorite place...the local dump. Velma would sit and read the Sunday paper while the boys examined the piles of rubbish, scouting for treasures to take home for the "fort" they'd dug out of their back yard. And, she would take off the month of August every year so she could take the family on a trip.

"Our clientele were the nicest people. I made some wonderful friends but everybody wanted me to be there all the time. If I was gone for a few days, they'd complain and go elsewhere saying 'Velma must not need the business.'"

Velma established a "kitty" with two of her friends, Opal Kennedy who owned three beauty shops, and Jane Guidi who worked for the Bakersfield Chamber of Commerce. Once a month, when there was enough money in the kitty, they'd take a weekend and drive to Las Vegas. "It would pay for the gas. We'd stay three to the room, go out dancing, and wear our pretty duds. They were fun times. Opal was a beauty! She's ninety-four now."

Jane Guidi approached Velma one day and said, "'the Bakersfield Junior College team had challenged the team from Boise Junior College to a football game', and we were to host the game. A group of business-men and dignitaries accompanied the team, and she wanted me to host a dinner for them. As busy as the restaurant was, I agreed to set up the Bailiff Room for them on Saturday night."

Many members of the Idaho contingent were Shriners, who arrived wearing tasseled red fezzes. "They were a happy bunch. One of them, who was pretty tipsy, asked me to come into the back room and meet the group. When I went back to greet them, the men were all smiling and shaking hands. One man stood out in the group. He was very distinguished.

He was white-haired, tall and handsome, with a gallant manner and the bluest, blue eyes I'd ever seen. His name was Harry Morrison and the tipsy man told me, 'he's quite a celebrity. He brought us down here in his plane.'

"When I learned that this was the very same 'Mr. Morrison' who founded Morrison-Knudsen, the company my sons' father worked for, I was astonished. Suddenly, the world shrunk a few more feet.

"My sons were with me since we were also going to the game. I'd bought them white windbreakers that afternoon, and they looked very sharp. Mr. Morrison complimented me on the restaurant and greeted the boys. When they shook hands with him, he gave each of them a silver dollar. They were thrilled.

"The men invited us to ride the bus with them. I said 'no' since we would be cheering for the other team, but the boys begged me to ride with them. Eventually, I relented and we rode to the game with the Boise contingent.

"It didn't make any difference where we sat that evening. It was so foggy you couldn't see the field anyway. The only way you could even tell that anyone had made a touchdown was because they had a cannon and you'd hear the gun go off. To this day I'm not even sure who won that game."

Chapter Six

A New Life Calls

The success of her restaurant brought Velma another opportunity. A new hotel was preparing to open in Santa Maria, and the owners asked her to run their restaurant. Before making a decision on it, she and her friend and business manager, Cora Leadbetter, made plans to go down to the coast and have a look at it in person.

Meanwhile, Harry Morrison had been stopping at Bakersfield from time to time, bringing his pilots into the restaurant. He always took time to visit with Velma. He would be going here or there to look over jobs, but somehow The Broiler always seemed to be on the way. A four-mile section of road at the Kern County Park consumed a great deal of his attention that year. In fact, he ended up personally supervising the project.

In later years Petra Asumendi, Mr. Morrison's personal secretary for thirty-eight years, told Velma that it was because of its proximity to her that such a small job assumed such important status, while other huge MK projects were ongoing around the world.

Trying to keep pace with the frantic life of the restaurant and her three growing children, Velma hadn't realized the attention being paid to her. So, she was surprised one day when she got a phone call from Mr. Morrison, inviting her and a friend to meet him for dinner in Santa Barbara when he went to the Sansum Clinic for a diabetes check-up. It was the same weekend she and Cora were going to Santa Maria, and she quickly agreed.

Harry sent a limo to pick up Velma and Cora and he took them to his favorite restaurant. Charmed by everything about him, Velma had a happy evening with Mr. Morrison. As dinner progressed, he said, "You know, I have a job out at Vandenberg Air Force Base that I need to check on tomorrow, but I need a good driver. Would you young ladies drive me over?"

Thrilled to spend another day with him, Velma happily accepted. He made arrangements to pick them up for breakfast. The weather was bright and blue. Fields of orange flowers stretched for miles as they drove toward Lompoc. Speculation about the bright flowers fueled their conversation for many miles. The beautiful blooms must be grown for seed, they decided. When they stopped for gas, they asked and found out that the flowers were ground into chicken feed and were the reason why egg yolks were colored such a bright yellow. "We laughed so hard over that.

We learn something new everyday. Sometimes it's more fun when you don't know the right answer to the questions," she said.

Arriving at Vandenberg Air Force Base, Harry presented his credentials to the guards at the front gate, and they were immediately accepted, but the guard refused to admit Velma and Cora to the base. "They're my guests," he insisted politely, but the young airman was not budging. "Please call the general and ask for clearance," Harry continued. Minutes later the general arrived in a Jeep and the ladies were escorted onto the base and welcomed royally.

For Velma, it was just a day's respite in the life of a busy working mother. The next day, she was back at the restaurant, totally immersed in the tasks at hand. "It was always busy, busy," she recalls.

The boys were growing and Judy was attending San Francisco State College. Some time later, Velma had another call from Harry Morrison. He was going to be in San Francisco to speak to the Associated General Contractors' convention and, knowing that Judy was in college there, he asked if Velma could make herself available to join him. "If you can accompany me, I'll send my plane for you."

Velma was very excited to be asked to meet him again, and she rushed home that night to tell her mother and grandmother, who offered to watch her boys. When she arrived in San Francisco, a limousine met her plane and whisked her to the Palace Hotel.

Her room was already arranged. Arriving upstairs, she was greeted by a vase of red roses, an orchid corsage and a lovely note welcoming her, saying he'd be there at 5:30 p.m. to pick up Judy and her.

"This is really something," Judy said, thrilled as she pinned on her mother's corsage.

Velma had bought a new dress for the occasion, something which she rarely did for herself. She and Judy were dressed in their finery, ready and very excited when Mr. Morrison arrived to take them to the dinner. When he first issued the invitation, Harry had told Velma that he'd be speaking at the dinner. Suddenly she found herself being seated next to him on the platform in front of a huge room filled with people in black tie and formal dress. "There probably were nearly as many people at the dinner as there were in the town where I grew up. This little old gal from Tipton, population 900, suddenly found her knees talking to one another. I was so shaken up. Even now, when I look back, I wonder how it all came about. I asked the waiter for an extra cocktail.

"I was totally shaken up. Mr. Morrison was six-foot, one inch tall. He had a stately manner, and he was so handsome. All I could feel was total admiration, total respect. I could hardly believe all of this was happening to me."

As he saw them to their room that night, Harry invited them to breakfast. "Is eight o'clock too early?" he asked. Since Judy had to leave early for school, that was a good time for her, so they all agreed.

The next morning, Velma and Judy were ready on time. Harry was a stickler for punctuality, so when he still hadn't arrived by 8:15, Velma, knowing he was diabetic, began to worry. They went down to his room and knocked on the door. When there was no response, they knocked harder. Velma dispatched Judy to find a maid to open the door. Entering his room, they discovered that Harry was passed out on the floor from insulin shock. The nursing lessons had prepared Velma for this moment. She ordered Judy to bring sugar and orange juice, and she forced it down his throat. Eventually, he regained consciousness and sat up.

"'You know, my boys have been wanting me to get a male nurse to travel with me and give me my insulin,' he said to me. Then he began to look at me. 'Now what the hell would I do with a male nurse?'"

Velma was back at The Broiler feeling like Pygmalion. She'd had a fabulous time in the company of Harry Morrison, but the restaurant was busier than ever, and her boys were growing fast. Between work and her children, there was little time to *think* about anything else. *Doing* took up all of her time.

Six months had flown by when Harry came into the restaurant with one of his pilots. "I've been thinking about you a lot," he said. "Do you think you could arrange to have dinner with me tonight?" Few things would have kept her from accepting his invitation. She quickly rearranged her schedule.

The conversation was light until they finished the meal. "The Broiler is a big business, and you work too hard," he said over dessert. "Have you ever thought you'd like to travel?"

Velma thought about the trips she'd made with her father when she was a child, and about the one she and Melva had taken to Venezuela. There were a few other trips she'd had an opportunity to enjoy, as well as the many dreams she'd had of traveling. Her ever-ready sense of adventure sprang to the surface. "I don't think about it much now, but I often did when I was younger. I'd love to travel when my children are grown."

"Let me make you a proposition," Harry said. "I need to find a nurse to travel with me. Whatever responsibilities you have, whatever your expenses, your salary will take care of that."

Thinking of her young sons, her daughter in college and The Broiler, Velma told him it just wasn't possible. Harry quietly persisted, "You ought to sell the business. If you can't sell it, you should just give it away. If you can't give it away, you should strike a match to it and burn it down." Despite her quick refusal, Velma continued to consider the offer.

"I talked to my mother and grandmother about the opportunity. 'Why do you have to come and ask us?' they answered me. 'It's a fabulous opportunity.' I was quite sure the salary couldn't cover my expenses, and I worried about selling The Broiler, the first business that finally was my very own. Still, I couldn't help but consider the offer at great length."

When Harry called to see if she had thought it over, she said, "Yes, I have. My mother and Tom have offered to take care of the boys when I travel, but they aren't young anymore and it's a lot of work. I can't ask them to do it."

"Why not?" he pressed. Hearing it was because of her sons, he persisted, "Henry Kaiser's grandson is in a military school at Redwood City. It's a boarding school. He loves it there. Your mother and Tom could pick them up on weekends."

With bits of the puzzle slipping into place, the idea gained feasibility. The thought of traveling and having to work fewer hours already had plenty of appeal. She put the business up for sale. It sold within minutes when an old friend and fellow restaurateur took her up on a long-standing offer to buy the Broiler if she ever decided to sell. "I'll be there in fifteen minutes," he said in response to her call.

Velma's house also sold quickly. She found a house in Burlingame for her mother, Tom and her sons. She frantically worked to complete the arrangements, but everything was working out on schedule.

Her time would be her own when she was not traveling, Harry said. Her first itinerary arrived. She would be gone for a month, visiting big banks and MK jobs all over North America. The itinerary was three pages long. "What have I gotten myself into this time?" she thought with trepidation.

Everything was in readiness until the day she got a call from her minister in Bakersfield. "I have something very serious to tell you," he said. "Someone from Boise called me a while ago and wanted to know what I knew about Velma Shannon. I answered all of his questions, and of course you came through with shining colors."

Velma was livid. How dare he be making calls to have her investigated?

The next time Harry called her, she vented her wrath. "How could you do that? How could you ask me to be your nurse if you were concerned about my character?"

Harry Morrison was speechless. He had no idea what she was talking about and said he had never had her investigated, but he thought he knew who might have done it. He'd check into the matter, he promised.

Knowing that he was a man of his word, Velma was satisfied. It turned out to have been a distant relative of Harry's late wife, Ann, who had called.

The plan was back on track.

Chapter Seven

Mr. Morrison

Harry W. Morrison was a tall, handsome man with courtly manners and a quiet, deferential way of making suggestions. He was well known for his hard work and personal integrity. By the time Velma met him, he was seventy-one years old, and well known throughout Idaho. The Morrison-Knudsen name was renowned the world over.

"It was a whole new world for me. Wherever we traveled, I was treated with such respect. On our first trip out of San Francisco, we stopped at Omaha, Nebraska to meet his friend and partner, Peter Kiewit to talk about a joint venture. Mr. Kiewit sent a car for us. He and Harry talked construction. I was included in all the lunches and dinners, but when I wasn't on the job, I got to go to all sorts of places. Mr. Morrison would pre-arrange sightseeing trips for me, or he would send the limo and I would go out with the wives of the local project managers.

"We also went to Vancouver, British Columbia. MK owned Northern Construction

Company. He would always check with all the personnel, and we would have big dinners every night. I was always met by wonderful people who kept me entertained while Mr. Morrison finished his work.

"When we went to Montreal, we were escorted to the 60th floor of the Bank of Canada. They welcomed Harry with open arms. It was all so amazing to me. The best stop of all was in New York City. The Waldorf Astoria was Harry's favorite hotel, and we had a huge suite. My room was filled with beautiful bouquets of fresh flowers. While he was visiting the company's headquarters in New York, I spent time with Dorothy Peavey, wife of Vice President Frank Peavey. We shopped and had a wonderful time while the men were working.

"Harry loved plays and the arts. We went out to dinner and saw all the best plays and productions. His favorite was Radio City Music Hall. He enjoyed the Rockettes and he just loved to watch all those leggy girls dance.

"After a while the big dinners began to take their toll on me. I must have puffed up like a toad. With the constant travel schedule, there just wasn't any way to work off all that good food.

"From New York we went to Chicago. There I began to feel like I'd made a really big mistake. This was not the life I wanted. It was a very heavy schedule, and I missed my children. It was getting close to Mother's Day, and I wanted to be home with my family.

"The next morning while having break-fast with Mr. Morrison, I broke the news. 'I've made a mistake. I want to go home. I'm sorry to tell you this, but this is not the right job for me.' Harry looked across the table in absolute shock as I continued, 'I can't go on with the itinerary. I have to go home.'"

His response was mild and, as always, considerate. "Perhaps I have been less than thoughtful about your time. I'll make arrange-ments for you to go home," he promised.

"I sat looking at him, thinking about how very fond I was of him. I admired his integri-ty. He had a marvelous way of treating peo-ple, and I cared deeply about him. I thought about how much I hated leaving, while at the same time feeling the overwhelming tug of my home and family.

"By 10 a.m., he'd arranged a first-class ticket and the limo was waiting to take me to the airport. As the plane flew into San Francisco, it was sunset, and I watched the glow over the city with feelings of sheer joy."

Another limo waited to take her home.

"By the time I'd had spent a week with my family, I was feeling much better. Then the papers arrived for the sale of my house in Bakersfield and The Broiler. Instead of just signing them and sending them back, I called Opal Kennedy, my boyfriend Dave, and Opal called her boyfriend Murray, to tell them I was coming for a visit. When I got there, the four of us went to the Stockdale Country Club for dinner, dancing and cocktails. We had a great time.

"Later, as we kicked off our sandals for the evening, Opal said, 'Velma, you've changed. Really changed.' And, for the first time, I began to realize that I really had changed during my trip with Mr. Morrison. Suddenly Dave seemed a little shallow, and things just didn't seem the same. My values, and the way I looked at men had changed.

"The next morning I signed the papers on The Broiler and my house, and caught my plane back to San Francisco. When I returned home, I was surprised to find Harry had sent me a beautiful bouquet of red roses with a note apologizing that he had not been more thoughtful about my time. He was apologizing to me? I was amazed!

"Harry said he'd be back in San Francisco soon and asked if I would meet him at the Fairmont Hotel for dinner. We always had a wonderful time together, and once again I thought about how much I enjoyed his company. Of course I'd meet him!

"So many things were tugging at my heart. When I was at home I yearned for more excitement, and I missed being with Mr. Morrison. When I was away on the itinerary with him, I missed my home and children.

"When we met at the Fairmont, he said he still needed me as his nurse, and he enjoyed my company. He said he would send the next itinerary and I could make corrections. He promised it wouldn't be as long. And he said

76

Ronnie, Gary, and Velma. "They were handsome little soldiers."

he loved my company. So, I returned to traveling with him.

"I guess it was just that I had to go home for a while and evaluate my lifestyle and my boyfriends. Once I'd been back, I realized there was nothing there. It wasn't there at all. But, if I hadn't gone back, I wouldn't have seen how different things were, and how different I had become. I had been exposed to a whole different world than I'd known.

"When I started traveling again, my whole attitude had changed. I began realizing that I had strong feelings about this wonderful man who treated me so well. I began to care very deeply for him. Today as I look back, I can't remember how many trips we made to MK jobsites around the country. He had so many companies, and there were MK partnerships all over the world. He wanted to visit all of them.

"As promised, Harry was more considerate of my time. I would sometimes find myself back in San Francisco with time on my hands. I had fun with my mother and my children, and would be home for two or three weeks at a time before going back out on trips. When my time at home had passed, I was eager to go again.

"When I had been traveling with Harry for about a year, he told me he was coming to San Francisco and offered to take me to dinner at the Fairmont Hotel. From across the room, I spotted him. Harry was so handsome, and my heart fluttered. 'What's happening to me?' I wondered.

"That night was an especially pleasant dinner. We really enjoyed being together, and we had grown comfortable with each other. He asked about my mother, grandmother, and the children. Then he asked me if I had ever thought about getting married again. 'No! I said emphatically.'"

"Well, I'd like to talk with you a little bit about that," he said gently. "Now, Velma, you really should marry a younger man than me, but you also might consider how I could help you and your family. You have led a very interesting life, and I will promise you one thing. The promise I will make to you is that if you marry me, you will never, ever be bored."

"Surprised and overwhelmed, I stalled, 'Well…I don't know. There are a lot of things involved,' I said, thinking mainly of my children."

"I don't need your answer right now," Harry said quietly, "but I'd like you to kindly think about it."

Velma's head spun. "Shortly before he proposed, Opal and I had been to Boise with Mr. Morrison. He introduced us to many of his closest friends. At an intimate dinner at the restaurant in the Owyhee Plaza Hotel, he had introduced me to his very closest friends. His lifelong best friend was Anna Hockberger. Anna also had been the best friend of Ann Daly Morrison, Harry's first wife. Anna's family had been at the dinner. Apparently, Harry had given the idea a great deal of thought before he asked me. Obviously I had been accepted and approved by Harry's inner circle of friends."

Velma knew about his background. He'd been recently widowed when she first met him. He and "Lady Ann" had been friends as well as husband and wife, and she had eagerly shared in his life of construction. Harry was in the midst of having Ann Morrison Park built in her memory and in her honor when Velma first met him. Ann was a wonderful woman, and she had been well loved in the community.

"Harry was born in central Illinois on February 23, 1885, near a homestead his grandparents had claimed. His father was a stationary engineer for a co-operative grain and seed company and he was a leader in the farmer's cooperative movement in that part of the state.

"Harry was four-years old, and his sister Edna was six and a half when their mother died. Shortly after her death, Harry contracted a rare form of appendicitis, and underwent surgery in his grandparents' farmhouse. It was a long, slow recovery. His father fashioned a cot that was put in the sunshine out in the back yard, and Edna lovingly supervised his convalescence."

As he began to regain strength, his cot was taken to his grandparent's house and he had a view of the construction of a railroad bridge over nearby Salt Creek. Young Harry struck up a friendship with the job superintendent, and he watched, admired and learned from this new friend.

He felt the sting of being considered less than his peers. Sent to a boarding school where students were divided into "haves" and "have nots," Harry fell into the group that was required to clean up after the wealthier students. It was an unforgettably uncomfortable feeling for him.

"He learned his work ethic early. He had to work summers to help with his support.

One summer he worked picking cherries, but he ate more than ended up in his bucket. He was fired. Another summer he worked behind a team of horses and a plow, but he decided almost immediately against that type of work. He knew there had to be a better way to make his livelihood.

"While he was still in his teens, he decided to leave school. Edna made him a generous loan from her piggy bank and, despite dire warnings from his father about his Uncle Ira who had run away to join the circus and had to borrow money to get back home, Harry was off to St. Louis to find his way in the world. Harry hadn't finished high school, but his old friend, the superintendent from Bates & Rogers that had built the railroad bridge during his convalescence, gave him a chance to work with a construction crew as the water boy. It gave him an opportunity to study people. He learned that those who didn't complain usually did the best work.

"Eventually Harry found his way to Idaho and was working on a reclamation project, the Minidoka Dam on the Snake River. His job was to dangle on a rope stretched high over the river and hand tools to the ironworkers. He did the job for a time, but decided it wasn't worth risking his life for what he was being paid. When he asked his supervisor for a raise, he was fired.

"Harry came to Boise and learned that a concrete inspector was needed for the Minidoka Project. The interviewing process would begin within days. Harry bolted for the public library to learn everything he could about cement and concrete. The next few days were a crash course on the topic, and Harry was ready for the interview. When he was asked if he knew anything about concrete, Harry won the job when he confidently boasted that he knew concrete 'from A to Z!'"

Back to the Minidoka site he went. When the old superintendent saw him, he growled, "you damned kid! What are you doing back here?" Harry calmly informed him that the tables had turned. The superintendent now was working for him, "and as long as you do your work all right, we'll get along just fine."

As he worked his way up the ladder and gained jobs with increasing responsibilities, he decided to talk with Morris Knudsen, a fifty-year old contractor with a team of horses he handled skillfully. "I'd like to go into business with you," he told Knudsen. Inquiring about what Harry would bring to the partnership, he replied, "plenty of guts." Knudsen said no, he'd meant how much money. Harry responded, "no money, just guts."

"That was how it happened that in 1912, Harry Morrison and Morris Knudsen founded the Morrison-Knudsen Company, which would grow to ultimately become the world's most prestigious construction and engineering firm. It was a partnership founded on a handshake, six hundred dollars, and a team of horses," Velma said.

On their first job, where they subcontract-
ed to build an irrigation pumping station on
the Snake River, the prime contractor got into
a legal dispute with the promoters. Despite
that, MK earned a small profit from the job,
but Harry also observed, "you can't make
money out of lawsuits." He walked away
from the experience with two lessons learned.
One was that if you had a job where a loss
had to be taken, you needed to do it on schedule and get on to the next job, always making
sure there was a next job. The second was that
he decided Karl Paine, the winning attorney in
the lawsuit, was someone he wanted on his
team. Paine became MK's first attorney and he
stayed with the company for many years.

Harry's sister Edna and her husband,
Howe Allen, relocated to Boise in 1911. The
Allens lived next door to the Daly family and
Harry soon became acquainted with Ann
Daly. Through her younger sister, he started
sending messages to Ann, but she thought he
was "too fresh." Harry, however, was nothing
if not persistent. He eventually talked Ann
into a buggy ride, but she didn't like his work
clothes and insisted he dress properly for the
ride. While his clothing was all right, his shoes
hurt too much for him to consider kissing Ann
goodnight. Nonetheless, the romance flour-
ished after its tentative start.

Leaving town on a job one day, Harry
presented Ann with the keys to his office and
asked her to take care of the mail while he
was gone. Flattered, she happily ran the office

in his absence. Sampling the construction life, she found she liked it and, while she often ended up splashed with mud and concrete, she eventually decided both the man and the life suited her.

Harry and Ann were married on December 12, 1914. Together they traveled the world and shared the construction life. Bridges, dams, canals, and highways were the foundation on which their partnership was built.

The business eventually became profitable. Harry educated himself through correspondence courses, night courses, and speech classes. He used crossword puzzles to stretch his vocabulary.

He pioneered the idea of the "joint venture" where several companies too small to tackle a large project on their own could become a consortium that could manage huge projects. The Hoover Dam, or the Boulder Dam as he preferred to call it, was the world's largest construction job at that time. The dam was successfully completed by the six companies that banded together to win the bid. They finished it ahead of schedule, within the bid, and with a profit to show for their efforts.

Not only did Harry think big, he expected the same of his employees. He reasoned that anyone who didn't think a job could be done didn't belong on that job. As the company tackled increasingly large projects, he had to devise a new system for tracking expenses so he'd always know whether the job would be profitable. His company developed a system of post-bid cost reports that would constantly show the profit or loss on the job.

He combined his work ethic with an acute eye for problem-solving and good relations with people. He could speed through the reports, spot trouble and take action immediately. He knew that staying in close touch with his employees helped them, and his system gave them the ability to turn losers into winners. Harry's frank, open way helped to develop tremendous loyalty among his employees. One employee, hired in 1932, later recalled how Harry would talk to him and tell him things he would have thought were company secrets. Later he found out Harry did that with other members of the company as well. People often worked for him for less money just because they liked the way he worked.

For employees who didn't need all of their wages during the busy season, he developed a system of payroll certificates. Employees received the same rate of interest on their certificates as they'd have received from a bank. When things were slow, they could trade in their certificates for cash.

Loyal to his employees, Harry also was loyal to business associates who helped him out. Left to cool their heels outside their banker's office one afternoon because they were dressed in dusty work clothes, he suggested to Knudsen that they "get the hell out of here." Needing money to meet payroll, they went across the street to Idaho First National Bank and introduced themselves to Crawford

Harry Winfield Morrison

Moore, the bank's founder. It was the start of a strong, enduring friendship. When the Great Depression forced the bank to close in 1932, Moore turned to Harry for help. Over Harry's protests that he was no banker, Moore prevailed upon him to help, saying, "people believe in you, admire you, and respect what you say."

Harry, although enmeshed in the Hoover Dam project, closed his own office, moved into the bank and led the reorganization committee's efforts. He personally handled the stock-sale canvassing. He stood on a box in front of the bank and convinced depositors to leave their money in the bank, telling them that if it failed, he'd give them each two dollars for every dollar they lost. He convinced the large, local companies that the sale was crucial to the future of the state, and they invested large portions of the needed cash. Taking a cue from the business leaders, people throughout the community rallied to help the bank and the campaign reached its goal in less time than anyone had thought possible.

As the company expanded to tackle jobs all over the world, Boise remained the company's home base. MK opened branches in key cities around the world. Harry traveled as needed, but he decided to leave the company's home base firmly anchored in Boise, which he considered his hometown.

Even with a life of constant work and travel, Harry still found ways to relax. He learned the lyrics to many western songs, and he'd sing them while picking out the tunes on his old guitar. He sang at company picnics and parties, always eager to have people laughing and enjoying themselves. He devoured detective novels. He loved Broadway shows and financed many productions, despite never finding a "hit." He loved baseball, and was an avid fan of the Boise Pilots, who later became the Boise Braves, a farm club for the Milwaukee Braves, and he always attended the games whenever he was in town. He loved the Boise Junior College football team. He purchased new team uniforms for the players, furnished instruments for the pep band, and he always told people, "When the band plays and the girls strut their stuff, *that* is when you have a college."

Time magazine called him a "master builder" when it placed his face on the cover of its May 3, 1954, issue, adding that Harry Morrison was "the man who has done more than anyone else to change the face of the Earth." *Business Week* and *Fortune* featured him in various issues as well, with similar accolades.

When Ann died in 1957, Harry was deeply affected by the loss of his beloved wife and friend. He began building Boise's beautiful Ann Morrison Park in her honor. The park wasn't a quick project. Starting without any particular plan, the ideas for it expanded as they went along. The park was still unfinished when Harry met, and later proposed to, Velma.

"When Harry proposed, I wondered how my children would react to my thoughts about marrying Mr. Morrison. And, I wondered about the park. How long would it take to finish and dedicate the park? I decided we'd have to talk about marriage another time.

Visiting a construction site. Harry made it a point to visit each company project.

"Still, I talked about the proposal with my family. My mother and sister again refused to give me advice on the issue. Then I talked to my children. Ron, who was 12-years old at the time, adamantly shouted 'no' as he stomped his foot on the floor, and told me he was the man of the house. Then he ran away.

"I found him later, crouched under a tree with his arms wrapped around his legs, and his head resting on his arms. His eyes were filled with great big tears, and my heart ached to see him so sad.

"'How would you like to go to Tijuana for a weekend?' I asked him. When he agreed, we made plans for the outing. We decided that we'd visit some of our family in Fresno, then head on to San Diego.

"Years earlier, I had taken Ron to a school in San Diego to work on his reading, and he

Ronnie, Velma, and Gary visiting Tijuana.

had grown to love the area. The outing in Tijuana gave us an entire weekend to talk. After all was said and done, Ron, somewhat grudgingly, gave his consent to my marriage. Judith was delighted. Gary was also fond of Mr. Morrison, and he made no objections, instead adopting a 'wait and see' attitude about the situation.

'When my next itinerary arrived, and I met Harry in San Francisco, I'd decided to accept his proposal. I would not marry him, however, until after Ann Morrison Park had been finished and dedicated.

"Harry moved the project into high gear."

The dedication monument in Ann Morrison Park.

Chapter Eight

A Wedding, a Honeymoon, and Boise

"One of Harry's very dear friends was J.K. Housells, a mining engineer he'd met while building the Boulder Dam. Housells later built the Tropicana Casino in Las Vegas. The dedication of Ann Morrison Park was set for late in June 1959, and our wedding date was set for July 1. Harry handled all the arrangements for the wedding and the reception through the Tropicana.

"There were no more itineraries as the days counted down toward the wedding. I was frantically making my own share of arrangements as well, with help from my mother and sister. On a shopping trip to San Francisco, I found the most beautiful blue lace dress I'd ever imagined. While Harry took care of the invitations for his family and friends, there were plenty I had to send out for my own side.

"Our whole family left from the Bakersfield Airport on the plane he'd sent for us. Grandma Lucy, Mother and Tom, Melva and Archie, my brother Earl and his wife Marilyn, Opal Kennedy, and my mother's sister, my Aunt Ann Taylor and her husband, Homer. With me, Judy, Ron and Gary we were ready for the short flight. The champagne flowed, and a limousine waited at the airport to take our party to the Tropicana. That night we had suites filled with flowers. We had a happy time at dinner and everyone enjoyed a floor-show.

"Mike Kennedy from the New York office, and his wife, Eleanor, were there with Harry. Mike was his best man. A large contingent of MK employees awaited us as we arrived at the Church of the Wildwood. Earl was going to walk me down the aisle. Melva stood by as my matron of honor. Suddenly, I found myself overcome by emotion. Big tears rolled down my cheeks. 'Don't you want to go through with it?' Melva asked me.

"'Oh yes…oh, I don't know.' So many thoughts flooded my head. I had been on my own for a long time. Yet I cared so much for Harry. I had been separated, but not divorced when I first met Harry, although I was divorced before I got to know him. That part felt odd. But I was very much in love with Harry Morrison.

"The question persisted: did I really want to be married again? Yes, I finally realized, I was ready. I loved Harry. I steadied myself, took Earl's arm and we started down the aisle.

"The ceremony went off without a hitch, and the reception following it was a grand celebration of our union.

Harry and Velma's wedding day, July 1, 1959

"When we first discussed our honeymoon, Harry had asked whether I'd like to go
to Honolulu. I was thrilled at the prospect. I'd
never been to Hawaii and was delighted to be
looking forward to a relaxing trip in a tropical
destination with my beloved husband. Mike
and Eleanor Kennedy accompanied us on the
trip. We stayed at the Hawaiian Village built

A Hawaiian honeymoon, arriving in Honolulu.

by Henry Kaiser. Henry was living in Hawaii, and he made all the arrangements for our entourage.

"The Kennedys had a suite at one end of the village, while we occupied the bridal suite. That evening, Alfred Alpaka sang the *Hawaiian Wedding Song* in our honor. As we sat snuggled under a trellis of spectacular tropical flowers, I thought surely I was in a dream.

"I kept thinking I'd wake up and find out that it had been a dream, that I'd been living in a fantasy. Harry was so handsome, so caring. It was a wonderful, unbelievable evening.

"The next morning, Harry asked Eleanor and me if we liked it there. 'Oh yes,' we

Mr. Morrison loved Hawaii.

enthused. We can shop and sunbathe and go out sightseeing."

Satisfied with their responses, Harry, Henry and Mike were off to tour MK projects while Velma and Eleanor were left on their own to do whatever they wanted. "It was just wonderful," Velma recalls, "until the third day. Then we started to wonder if they were ever coming back. Harry did call intermittently, but the men were gone for days."

Eleanor proved to be a good friend to Velma. Eleanor was very proper. When they

Harry and Henry Kaiser

first met in New York, Harry had asked her to "show Velma the ropes." Eleanor was able to teach Velma, the little farm girl from Tipton, a bit about this sophisticated new world that she'd never seen before.

Eleanor was very fashionable. They became good friends, and she showed Velma around the big city. "When I was younger, I never expected to find myself in such a place. Everything was different from what I grew up with. I'll tell you how naivé I was," she says, "the first time we went out to lunch and

Eleanor ordered vichyssoise for us, I had no idea that I'd be getting cold potato soup."

Back from the honeymoon, Velma got her first taste of life in Boise. "I wondered what people would think of me in Harry's home town. He and Ann were both well loved here, and I was a newcomer; some thought that I was an intruder.

"He was 'Mr. Morrison,' founder of the largest construction company in the world. Everything about him was just right. That is why I had grown so fond of him. That's why everyone loved him and respected him. But I had only been here to visit, and now I had chosen to live in Boise.

"When I arrived here, Harry had a house-keeper. She immediately announced that she wasn't taking orders from some new lady, and she quit. It was just as well, the house needed attention, so she obviously hadn't been doing that much work anyway."

Velma rolled up her sleeves and dove into the needed tasks. She went to the store and bought cleaning supplies. The man at the counter was friendly. "One of the first things that struck me about Boise was the attitude people had wherever I went. They were so friendly; they just seemed happy and jovial. Being from California, I wasn't used to having strangers smile at me and be so friendly.

"With my supplies in hand, I went home, tied a red bandanna around my head and got busy cleaning up the house. Soon there was a knock on the door. Two women were there.

Our house at 912 Harrison Blvd.

They wanted to welcome me to the neighborhood. I was in dungarees and had on my apron and bandanna. I welcomed them and invited them into the house.

"One of their first questions was, 'are you going to be living here?' and they said they were surprised because we could have had the nicest house in town. After a few minutes, they had asked so many questions I wondered why they had even stopped in, but they said they wanted to be good neighbors. I just wanted the nosey old biddies to go away. I thought about offering them a cup of tea or coffee, but since I didn't know what they wanted yet, and was hoping they'd go away, I didn't make the offer.

A Karsh photo of Mr. Morrison.

"When Harry came home that night, I'd
fixed a little dinner for us. He was talking
about a trip around the world. We hadn't
done that before, but he wanted to go and
check on all of the company's projects. I was
ready to travel, so he started working on our
itinerary. It was comforting to think about

101

Composite photo for Harry Morrison's 80th birthday

traveling with him again. I was finding that it wasn't easy to come here from outside and be accepted by the community as the wife of a giant. With him busy preparing the itinerary, I

On tour in
Tokyo while
visiting projects
in Japan

Visiting Rio de
Janeiro and
our Brasilian
projects

spent my time getting the house in shape. I was in the house for several weeks before I finally discovered the last bathroom."

Before their marriage, all of their travels had been within North America. Now they were going to travel the globe. "I was excited about going around the world," Velma said. "I can't remember all of the places where our first itinerary took us. It included Central America and Honduras, since our company was building the Pan American Highway. We saw various jobs and met all of the project managers.

"We went to Nicaragua, then were off to South America. We landed in Venezuela, and Harry said, 'you know, we built the most expensive highway ever built.' It went from sea level all the way to Caracas (elevation 3,105 ft.), and it cost seven million dollars a mile back in 1959.

"We saw the Oronoco River job, which was a large dam. I told Harry I had been there before. The project manager met us at the airport. There was the skin from an anaconda on the arch over the entry to the camp. It was huge! Harry knew everyone. He asked about the manager's wife and kids. And in our company newsletter, the EmKayan, he'd say nice things about how hard working the wives were on the construction projects. He always said the wives were to be commended for their courage, dedication and loyalty. They kept everything going. After I saw that huge

On the yacht of Ferdinand Marcos. "To show off, he showed me he could water ski on one foot with no skis."

snakeskin, I agreed that they sure should be commended! It was unbelievably large.

"As time went on, I found more and more things to love and admire about Harry. If a man was hurt on a project, he would always call the wife and family to see what they might need. He'd always try to be helpful. They took precautions, but in spite of everything they did, accidents would happen.

"From Caracas, we went on to Brazil. The company had been working on numerous projects in South America for about thirty years, and there was a company headquarters in Rio. Morrison-Knudsen built the infrastructure for Brasilia, and it had built three big dams around Brazil. An agreement with the Brazilian government said foreign companies couldn't take profits from large projects out of Brazil. Only a percentage of the money could leave, most of it had to be reinvested within the country.

"Then we went on to Buenos Aires, the 'Paris of South America,' where we were met by Henry Kaiser, who had an auto plant nearby in Cordova. That was where the Kaiser automobiles were being built. Most of the Kaisers were sold within South America. It was the only brand of vehicle being manufactured on the continent, which offered a great, growing market and the company was charged no taxes.

"Buenos Aires is very much like Paris. It is very French. Henry took us out to dinner at a beautiful café with checkered tablecloths. It was a pleasant, balmly night. The two men were very fond of one another. They had worked together since they built the Boulder Dam back in the 1930s. They'd been together through the shipyard days during the war.

"This trip was just after the Russians invaded Hungary. There were many Hungarians in the area, and many violinists wandered through the restaurant playing for us. Harry and Henry kept putting money in their pockets, asking them to keep playing for us. They played

Velma and Harry at Mr. Morrison's office.

until 2 o'clock in the morning. They kept begging us, 'please take us back to North America with you. We'll play for you all the time.'

"The next day Henry took us to see his automobile plant. It was a beautiful day. The weather was ideal. It was in the rolling pampas country, and the people were friendly.

"From there we went to Chile where we were building copper mines, and our plane flew high up over the Andes. It was so high! I had caught a terrible cold and just wanted to come home. My head was aching, and the planes back then were not pressurized as well as they are now. I was so happy when we were back on the ground.

"There were more big dinners. Everyone wanted to meet the boss. One night Harry was hurrying me to be on time. I said, *'I'm not going!'* I wanted a doctor to give me something for my sinus headache. He ended up going to the dinner alone. Still, he wanted me to come along, and he said we had to go to Ecuador, to keep to the itinerary. I was too sick to keep going. He pushed and pushed. I stayed in the hotel. I didn't see the job, and I didn't go to the dinner. We flew home on the Pan American Clippers. They had beds so you could sleep on long flights. I was so glad when we landed in Los Angeles!

"Talk about adventures! I've had more than my share. Mr. Morrison was my mentor, and he taught me well. I still remember almost everything he taught me and everything about the time we spent together.

"Harry just never took 'no' for an answer. Nothing was impossible to him. If it could be done, he would see that it would be done."

Chapter Nine

Horsing Around

Velma was fascinated with horses from her earliest days. The huge, sleek creatures were integral to the farm setting where she grew up, but the work horses around the farm were peasants compared with the regal, high strung horses found in Thoroughbred racing.

The Mitchell Ranch and Gem State Stables

Velma and Melva near the little farmhouse where they grew up.

"When Harry and I started Gem State Stables on Grandmother Mitchell's old farm in the early 1960s, it was fortunate that we were able to hire my brother Earl who had a great deal of experience with horses. He'd been training them and racing them for a long time, so he became our trainer and business manager. He had been an associate of Lucille Ball and Desi Arnez and the stables they owned in Corona, California, where they bred and raced Thoroughbreds.

"Earl had been in the business long before I caught the fever. One time Harry and I were invited to visit Lucy and Desi's farm. Harry was ecstatic. He'd long been a huge fan of Lucy's. We began talking about horses.

"Some time after that, we were in New York at the Waldorf when a page boy came through the lobby calling out, 'Call for Mr. Morrison. Call for Mr. Morrison.' It turned out to be Earl on the phone."

"Well, Harry, Velma's birthday is coming up. I have an idea for the perfect present for her," Earl announced.

"Somewhat skeptically, Harry said to him, 'Oh yeah? What's that?'"

"Earl explained that there was a special mare going up for auction. It was one of Queen Elizabeth's mares, named Barbette. She was with foal, and the sire was a famous stallion. The auction would be at Santa Anita Park, and it was a 'package' deal. The foal came with the mare. It seems like it was going to be $11,000, and it sounded like quite a bargain for the start of a horse farm.

"Mr. Morrison mentioned that we didn't have a horse farm *yet*, and asked, 'Where would we put them?' Earl said we could keep it at Lucy and Desi's farm until we decided what to do. When Harry told me about the idea, my mind started racing.

"That mare was the start of our stables. For a while it was all right having the horses at Lucy and Desi's farm, but we had to send a big upkeep check each month. When the foal was born, we had to send big checks for both horses. Being the mercenary girl that I am, I figured it was time to start our own ranch."

Velma and Harry Morrison with California Governer
and Mrs. Pat Brown

Grand opening of Gem State Stables

The Elk's Band from Boise at the grand opening of the
Gem State Stables

Since Velma was dreaming of owning her
own horse ranch, Harry told her during a visit
to her farm, "Grandmother Mitchell's old farm
house will have to go. And, we'll have to
build a little barn. "

"While I wasn't there, he made plans for a
whole new arrangement. He built a new
house, stables, and no small barn — it was a
big barn with 16 stalls, eight on each side. And
we had a house for the veterinarian, bunkhouse
for other employees and other outbuildings.
Using MK equipment, he put in new concrete
ditches and surprised me with them as well as
a new house on the site.

"There were three governors at the grand
opening of the Gem State Stables. The governors of Idaho, California and Montana all

Harry and Velma Morrison at the grand opening of the Gem State Stables

came to it. There were five hundred people there. People from Tipton who knew me when I was growing up were really surprised, and they were thrilled to be invited to the party! Our stables were quite a thing for Tulare County.

"In the meantime my niece, Argene, asked me to go with her to a horse sale in Lexington, Kentucky. She wanted to upgrade our brood stock. We were put up in the Campbell House where we looked through catalogs. Then we went down to look at the horses. Early the next morning, there was a tap on our door, and my brother Earl said we

Brother Earl and Velma at the opening of The Mitchell
Family Chapel in Tulare, California. Harry and Velma
built the chapel for the Mitchell Family.

needed to go down to see this yearling colt we wouldn't believe, sired by Bold Ruler.

"I said 'no!' We don't need a yearling! We need brood mares. I checked through the catalogs again, and then on my own I went down to see Bold Ruler's colt. Argene and I had an attendant bring out the colt. He was a beautiful specimen. We were so excited. I didn't tell my brother about it, but I had a friend, Jim Camp, who lived twenty minutes from my ranch who knew horses and did sulky racing.

"I called him to come out and look at the colt, and he said he'd buy it with me. I told him it went on the block the next night, and he flew his plane to Kentucky. I met him at the airport. After Jim looked at the horse, he said it would go for far too much money. The bidding started at five thousand dollars and quickly jumped up to seventy thousand dollars. It was down to two bidders. A yearling had never gone for that much money before.

"I said to myself, 'so you're a chicken now? You want to start a horse ranch and you're afraid to buy what will put you on top.' For a long time we'd been looking for property around Payette Lake. I decided to give up the house on the lake and shouted 'One hundred eighty thousand dollars! *Give me the horse.*" The auctioneer was saying, 'going once…going twice…' and I shouted, *'give me the damned horse!'*"

The auctioneer called out, "Sold to the lady in red!"

Velma said, "There goes my house on the lake!" She chuckles at the memory. "Today yearlings sell in the millions, but that was the most ever paid for a yearling at that time. My hands were shaking so hard I could barely sign the tab for it. My brother said, 'What have you done now?'" Velma said, "'You really wanted that colt, didn't you?'"

"I answered yes, but not at that price!

"By this time it was late at night, but I thought I'd better call my husband and let him know what I did. I was afraid that if I didn't let him know right away, he'd hear it on the news before I had a chance to tell him. I called Harry and told him I'd bought the horse with one bid. He wasn't surprised at that. 'So what else is new?' he asked me. I told him how much I'd paid, and there was a long silence at the other end of the phone.

"'You didn't get there by yourself, did you?' he asked.

"My brother Earl wanted to syndicate the horse, but I didn't want to. Earl didn't wait for me. He arranged for the syndication while I was deciding whether that's what I wanted to do. There were thirty-two shares, and I owned seventeen of them. With the sale of the shares, we got all of our money back and the account was settled."

The new yearling, now named One Bold Bid, was shipped to his new home in California. Velma had her start on the dream of a horse ranch. When she and Harry went to the train station to pick up the colt as he arrived in

Velma and One Bold Bid

Arcadia by boxcar, a man in business attire met the Morrisons. "He came up to Harry and told him he was from the California Tax Commission. He said there was six percent sales tax due on the purchase. He gave us a bill for $10,800 in sales tax!

"As it turned out, One Bold Bid was a total dud. We kept him as a yearling, but when he was a two-year old we realized he couldn't handle training. He was too stocky. We took him to University of California-Davis where they told us he had bad knees, bad everything. He never did race. He was sold as a stud. It was lucky for me that Earl had sold shares.

"Mr. Morrison liked horses, and he loved to go to the races. He couldn't wait until the

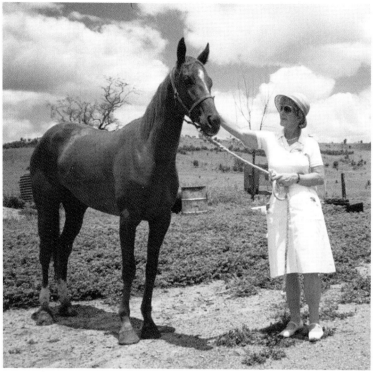

Velma with Fast Fellow, the Thoroughbred from Gem State Stables

next race, where he'd place two-dollar bets on his favorite horses. It just tickled him to watch the races, and he was ecstatic when he won.

"Our stables grew like Topsy. From that very small beginning, in just a few years, we were the second largest breeder of Thoroughbreds in the state of California. We had eighty-two brood mares of various pedigrees, thirteen stallions which were owned in shares by different people, and a full-time veterinarian. It was a full working ranch.

119

"We got to know so many interesting people during those years. We met the Guggenheims from New York City, Elizabeth Arden Grimm, and many famous horse breeders.

"We had one spectacular horse in our stable named Fast Fellow. I was very fond of him. We had just flown into the ranch one day in January and the vet said, "I'm glad you're here. We have two mares ready to foal tonight. I said, 'oh good, be sure to call me on the intercom when it's time.'

"The intercom in our room squawked during the wee hours, and the vet said, 'Mrs. Morrison, the foal is coming any minute.' I slipped on a coat and boots and went straight to the barn. When I ran outside and into the warmth of the barn, there he stood on wobbly legs, and his mother was cleaning him up. He was darling, and I said, 'My gosh, he's such a fast fellow!' The name stuck.

"Although we were involved with the racing and breeding, we always put the yearlings up for sale. That next year I looked in the catalog, and Fast Fellow was not in there. When I asked Earl about it, he said he'd had his eye on him to keep for our stables. ***He was so right!***

"Fast Fellow went on to be a big name and he made our Gem State Stables very well known. One time Earl called me and wanted me to come out and watch his training workouts. It was at Santa Anita, and there were many two-year olds there. We watched him and were very excited. He had very fast times, and we were so encouraged.

"His training went beautifully, and he was nominated to run in the Hollywood Handicap, a race for two-year olds. It was a big day and a big race, with a $100,000 purse for the winner. We had our whole family there, and Mr. Morrison and I took the company plane filled with MK executives to watch the big race. It was so exciting.

"We could hardly wait for the eighth race when Fast Fellow would run.

"Would you believe that Fast Fellow won first place? I was so shaken up I couldn't even stand up to walk down to the Winner's Circle. It took quite a while before I was able to stand at all, and my knees were shaking when I went down to get our award. Alfred Hitchcock was the presenter, and he gave us the prize, an engraved, solid gold loving cup.

"Fast Fellow went on to win many races for us. He was an amazing, wonderful horse. He won his races at Saratoga in New York, Arlington Park in Chicago, and other parks.

"When he was eligible to race in the Kentucky Derby as a three-year old, I was ecstatic to think about how we had bred and raised a horse to run in the Derby. My brother had other thoughts, however. He told me as gently as he could that Fast Fellow was not going to run in the Kentucky Derby. He said the horse couldn't do the length, he was a sprinter. He said he wouldn't put him in the race and risk having him hurt.

"I told him in no uncertain terms that Fast Fellow was going to race in the Kentucky Derby. He was eligible, and I wanted to see him there.

"My brother gave me an ultimatum at that point. He said if Fast Fellow ran in the Derby, it would be with another trainer. I was shocked and so hurt, but eventually I accepted his decision. He was correct. He knew his horses.

"But, Fast Fellow's saga continues. True to his name, he was very fast. Breeders of quarter horses wanted to purchase him to service their mares. We received an offer we couldn't refuse from a man who was a breeder and a well-known veterinarian, and Fast Fellow moved to Oklahoma.

"Several years later I was in Oklahoma City checking on a large MK project where we were building a General Motors plant. After visiting the jobsite, I asked the driver to take me to the vet's home and farm to see how Fast Fellow was doing. As we got near, I could see him, standing high on a hill with all of his mares contentedly grazing around him. I have a beautiful picture of him in my mind. It's like a video. He ended up having a very good life. That was the last time I saw him.

"Once we went to Ireland to buy a horse with a fabulous pedigree. He was a two-year old we wanted to race and have for stud. His name was 'Gay Challenger' and he had fancy bloodlines. We had him flown from Ireland to California, and then shipped by rail to our stable in Tulare. Some time later, we were shipping him from our ranch to New York to run. On the way he had some kind of fit and injured himself. He broke his right, front leg.

"You have to have lots of heart to survive in the racing business. Racing is a challenge but it's also a joy.

Chapter Ten

Married Life

Velma was happy. She was married to a man who treated her with great respect, and he loved her children. He treasured her company, her sense of humor and her insight. "Mr. Morrison was my mentor," she often says, but it also is apparent that for all he taught her, he greatly respected and appreciated her ideas and perspectives. Velma brought great joy to his life.

Now married, their itineraries became longer and trips were frequently outside of the United States. Velma quickly became a seasoned world traveler. "Mr. Morrison was always punctual. If he said we were leaving at 8 o'clock, you had better be there beforehand. You surely didn't want to be even a minute late. If people weren't there on time, he left them."

The stops were occasionally hair–raising, but for the little farm girl from Tipton, they were always fascinating. On one trip when they were in Istanbul, Turkey, they were caught in the midst of a revolution. They spent three days in a hotel, out of food and low on water. John Foster Dulles, the United

Christmas on Harrison Blvd.

States' Secretary of State, also was in the hotel.
He eventually managed to arrange for a 3:30
a.m. Lufthansa flight to get them out of the
country. " Velma said to Harry, " Hear those
guns? We're all going to be killed! The bus
broke down on its way to the airport, but the
driver came to the rescue, tinkered with the
engine a while and got it started again."

In later years, on another journey, Velma's
son Ron accompanied her to inspect a dam

that was being built in Zaire. Ron wanted to go out in the jungle to see the gorillas. There were only about 370 mountain gorillas left at that time, and they had been the subjects of intense study. The group leader informed them that Cashmere was the head gorilla, and he was huge. There was to be no talking or loud noises as they walked the trail toward the gorillas' territory.

By the time they had walked for an hour, Velma was tired and decided to head back for the bus. She left unnoticed by anyone in the group, and had gone some distance before she realized that the trail had closed in behind her in either direction. Suddenly she became acutely aware of the cacophony of wild sounds in the jungle, and she considered an encounter with a black mamba or a green mamba, snakes that were both plentiful and deadly. Branches lashed her face as she walked. The skies opened and torrential rains soaked her to the skin. Eventually she spotted a long wisp of smoke and followed it to a hut occupied by a pygmy, who invited her into his tiny home fashioned from mud, sticks and stone.

"He crushed tobacco in his hands, found a smidge of paper and rolled a cigarette. I smoked, he smoked. About an hour and a half later, they came along and found me. The man from Belgium who was leading the tour sure gave me hell."

On another long itinerary with Harry, they made a stop in Venezuela. They were met by a car in Caracas, and again went to view construction on a new dam on the Oronoco River. "It was a huge project!" Velma recalls. "I was issued my hard hat and we went right down there. It was a fabulous project to view. Even though we'd done many big projects, it was so mammoth I was overwhelmed. The scope of the entire project was gigantic. I ran out of adjectives to describe it.

"We toured all the different areas, and Mr. Morrison greeted everyone and shook hands with them. We were wearing heavy boots, and we got very dusty and dirty by the end of the day. When they took us to our quarters, the arch that greeted us was covered with an anaconda skin. It had to be well more than twenty feet long. The foreman told us they were plentiful around there. I was afraid to go to sleep!"

Morrison-Knudsen was contracted after World War II to build many projects throughout the Middle East. The company had already been in Iran for more than thirty years, and had ongoing jobs throughout Afghanistan, Iraq, Turkey and Pakistan. Roads, dams, bridges and a huge steel mill were among the projects they built.

"On one trip through Pakistan, Harry went into insulin shock because I had lost track of the time changes as we traveled back and forth across time zones. We were in Lahore, Pakistan checking on a road project. We had been out viewing jobs and I lost track of the time. It turned out that I'd been giving him his insulin injections without adjusting for all the time changes.

"Mr. Morrison was severely diabetic. It was a very bad reaction. Fortunately, there were excellent doctors connected with the project. He had several days of rest, medication and fluids before he was back on the job, and then you couldn't stop him or slow him down. Despite his diabetes, he was a man of unusual stamina and determination.

"When we were back at work, I went out and rode camels with the wives of the other men on the project."

One big change after the episode with the insulin shock was that the Morrisons decided to have a doctor travel with them when they were heading out alone to foreign countries. From that time on, Dr. Hildahl Burtness, who was in charge of the Sansum Clinic in Santa Barbara, and his wife Luella began accompanying them on their bi-annual overseas trips.

Velma said the company always believed that its representatives should accept local hospitality as it was offered, without complaint. MK did not allow its employees to be "ugly Americans." As a result, she also learned to adapt to all types of conditions. "I don't remember which project, but it was in Iraq. We were way out in the desert, and we stayed in a small village. Toilets were a hole in the ground. You just sat on the ground over the hole with your feet stretched out in front of you. That was outside of Baghdad, and fortunately, we only had to do that once."

For all of her travels, one of the most memorable sights for Velma was the Taj Mahal in India. "At the time there weren't many buildings that were air-conditioned, but the car had air-conditioning. We went to India to see a dam the company was building.

"Everywhere we went there were thousands of people on bicycles. We turned down one street in New Delhi, and there were tantalizing smells coming from pits where chicken was being cooked over coals. We stopped to eat, and we were served big bowls of rice with raisins, curry and the chicken. It was wonderful food!

"There were so many people wherever we went in India — children of all ages, adults, grandparents who looked ancient. Cows were wandering everywhere. All of those places, all of those things are still wonderful memories for me.

"There were so many trips over the years. We built the bridge over the Tagus River in Lisbon, Portugal. It was a spectacular project. John Armitage was the project manager. He picked us up at 5:30 in the morning from the Ritz Hotel in Lisbon, and took us down to show us all the tugboats working on the project. He took us out on his small boat that he used to get back and forth.

"He told us 'one tugboat is named the *Henrietta* in honor of the wife of Lyman Wilbur, who was the most prestigious engineer who ever worked at MK. Another was named the *Marie* in honor of Marie Bonny, wife of MK president Jack Bonny." The tour continued. "This tugboat," he concluded, "is called the *Velma*, and it works harder than the

Entertaining MK employees in Lisbon, Portugal.

other two put together." As we've worked on her memoirs, Velma always has to stop for a good laugh at this point.

The travel, despite its hardships, suited Velma. She found herself learning and growing. She deeply appreciated the variety of experiences, "each country was different, and each had things to enjoy. The world is full of wonderful cultures. I liked all of them for different reasons. Life is truly an adventure."

In her own country too, Velma found much to love, and many differences. She returned to the Alaska she had met in her youth. The former student nurse came to mar-

The Velma M

vel at the mountains, the wild rivers, the vast spaces, the diverse wildlife, and she enjoyed helping to be part of the construction of the Alaska Pipeline that would bring oil wealth and relative economic stability to the Great Land. Historically, Alaskans struggled along through a pendulum of "boom and bust" economic cycles. The money from the oil pipeline helped smooth out economic wrinkles in Alaskan life. She loved Prudhoe Bay and Valdez.

"All of America is so full of scenic treasures," she says with wonder. "In California, you can stand on Highway 395, look down at Death Valley, the lowest spot in the United States, and look up at Mt. Whitney, the highest peak in the Lower 48. Utah has amazing rock formations. The Navajo people have a language and culture unlike anyone else's. At the Four Corners, you can stand with your feet in Utah, Colorado, New Mexico and Arizona at the same time."

A true citizen of the world, Velma will tell you, "Hawaii, the South American Andes, Antarctica, Mexico, Idaho, India...it doesn't matter where you travel, it's all so different, all so beautiful."

Being with Mr. Morrison, enjoying his company and he hers, "I found life very freeing. I could just be myself when I was with him, and I found myself working harder than I'd ever worked before. There was so much I was learning!

"I never did the tiniest iota for Mr. Morrison that he didn't say 'thank you.' Even when I'd give him his insulin shots, he'd always say, 'Thank you, Vel.' Mr. Morrison made fifty thousand dollars a year and never thought about his income. I say this often, but he really was a great mentor for me. I have applied what I learned from him to my own businesses, including my farm and managing the Morrison Foundation.

"Morrison-Knudsen was the best at what it did. It also was frequently the first. We were

At the MK office in South America

the first company to build missile silos during the Cold War. The first was near Denver, and it was deep underground. You had to take elevators to go down to it. The magnitude of all of it was mind-boggling.

"We built the vertical assembly building at Cape Kennedy, now Canaveral, and it was the size of four football fields. It housed the space modules that took our antronauts to the moon. We also built the Houston facility for NASA, the National Aeronautics and Space Administration. That was something! There were water moccasins everywhere. Around there you quickly learned to turn your boots upside down at night. Our engineers said the snakes even got into the engines of their pick-

Harry Morrison's 80th birthday. He knew as a youth
that he did not want to follow a plow.

up trucks. Despite the hardships along the
way, it was very exciting to be part of it.

"We built the Metro system in Washington,
D.C. We worked on the St. Lawrence Seaway
project in Quebec. We worked on the largest
projects in the world, and we traveled constantly."

The fifteen years of their marriage sped
by all too quickly. They were years when
Velma began to appreciate superlatives for the
way they helped to describe the scope of the
company's projects.

But, Mr. Morrison's health was slowly
declining. "God was good to us. Harry lived

Harry Morrison and his sister, Edna Morrison Allen, were lifelong friends and companions. Harry reached the age of eighty-six. Edna lived to celebrate her 104th birthday.

to be eighty-six, even though he was diabetic. What wrenched my heart the most was seeing him slowly lose the ability to walk and having to go to a wheelchair. We were always trying to keep his mind active. We'd go to places he was fond of, and take lots of small vacations. He loved scenic views. We'd go to the diabetes clinic in Santa Barbara. And he loved to go to the races."

Left to right, back row: Velma, Gladys, and Earl. Front row: Harry, Melva, and Earl's wife Marilyn.

During the four years he was in a wheel-chair, Velma had two male nurses who helped her care for him. "Even through all of that, he never lost his sense of humor. He never complained. He always was so gracious and so grateful to those who cared for him.

Edna and Velma on Edna's 100th birthday

"He always loved the railroads. I used to take him in the car, and we'd drive down to watch the trains. And he loved baseball. Jim Brown, publisher of the *Idaho Statesman*, owned the baseball team, and Harry sponsored it.

"We had invitations to go everywhere, but he got to where he was unable to go places. Most of his friends gradually stopped coming around. He always said you could count your true friends on one hand without needing the thumb or the little finger. Vern Otter, J.R. Simplot and Don Daly were always his faithful friends. It broke my heart and

Front row, left to right: J. B. Bonny, Harry Morrison, and Burt Perkins. Second row: Lyman Wilbur and Mr. Olmstead.

frightened me to watch him fading day by day.

"Sometimes I'd say to Mr. Morrison, 'Harry, did you ever realize what you started?' He'd smile, and I would start to name the companies he'd built: Morrison-Knudsen, National Steel & Shipbuilding, HK Ferguson

Company in Cleveland, River Construction Company in Fort Worth, National Engineering in San Francisco… there were so many more.

"During his later years, we often talked about what my life would be like after he was gone. He told me to watch out for gigolos, especially those who'd curl their mustaches around. We'd laugh, but it was difficult to think about those things. We were happy together. It was very hard to see his health going downhill. It wrenched my heart that he couldn't do the things he loved.

"His sister, Edna, lived to be 104-years old. She had a wonderful outlook on life, and she loved being around young people. They returned her love. She had a vast store of wisdom. She and Harry were lifetime companions. She had taken care of him, and he always saw to her welfare."

For fifteen years, Velma had been loved, and had learned about the world. Harry Morrison had been her mentor, her husband, her companion and her friend. All too soon, he was gone.

"After Mr. Morrison died in 1971, everything changed. Among other things, I decided to have a dispersal sale and get rid of the horse business. It wasn't the same without him. We did very well over our ten years of racing, breeding and selling, but that chapter of my life closed when Mr. Morrison passed away.

"Then one more sad thing happened during that time. I had a beautiful stallion named

Imbros and his little goat

Fast Fellow

Imbros. He came from famous bloodlines. He was a magnificent animal, and the sire of Fast Fellow, but he was very high strung.

"Imbros had a little goat who was his best friend. The little goat always stayed with him in his stall in the stable. If Imbros was lying down, the little goat would walk all over his stomach or curl up with him. When Imbros went to the breeding barn, the little goat went right along with him. The goat went wherever Imbros went. They were inseparable companions.

"When I had the dispersal sale, Imbros was bought by our friend Bob Fluor, who was the founder of Fluor Corporation, another world-renowned engineering and construction company. I was very fond of that horse, and Mr. Fluor had paid a pretty penny for him. I decided to go along on the three hundred fifty mile trip in the van when we delivered him to Mr. Fluor's stables.

"I told his stableman about Imbros and the goat and said that they should never be separated under any circumstances. I told him they'd be fine in the stall together, but that they always had been together, and they couldn't be apart.

"Well, he didn't listen to me. I don't know what became of the little goat, but they were separated. Imbros killed himself by running his head into the barn wall and throwing himself around until he was so badly injured that he died. I never understood why the man at the stables did that."

Chapter Eleven

Single Again

Once again, Velma found herself on her own. Mr. Morrison was gone, but Velma was left to carry on his legacy. She remembered being the little country girl whose knees "talked to each other" the first time she sat on the dais next to Mr. Morrison at a major event, but that little girl was gone. There had been tumultuous changes in her life. She had lived and worked on the world stage. She had traveled much and learned more. She had dined with princes, potentates, captains of industry and a host of movie stars. With the help of Mr. Morrison, her beloved husband and mentor, she had discovered a deeper love and respect than she'd ever known before, and she had received valuable guidance. Velma learned her lessons well, and now she was confident she could find her own way.

Velma continued to travel the world. She'd been tested, and had proven her mettle. She visited far-flung MK jobsites, and was an active member of the board of directors for

Velma with Carly Zell

Morrison-Knudsen. She also oversaw and continued the work of the Morrison Foundation,
which had been started many years before by
Harry and Ann Morrison.

One day in the mid-1980s, Velma received
a call from John Hockberger. John's mother,
Anna, had been a lifelong friend to Harry, Ann
and Edna. John, and his late wife Rosemary,
had attended Velma's first dinner in Boise,
when Harry had brought her and Opal to
town to meet his friends and acquaint her
with the company.

Pleased to hear from her old friend,
Velma settled into a chair to enjoy his call.
John was the chairman of a local water dis-
trict. He discussed the energy shortage, of

which Velma was aware, and he discussed the hydropower that was available but was going to waste. He wanted to see the water used for power. The Lucky Peak Dam belonged to the members of his water district, and John had decided it should be used for more than merely irrigation.

The district had talked with Idaho Power. The farmers had their bonding and were all ready to sign contracts with the utility. But they hit a snag when they discovered that the company was not willing to pay enough money for the power to make the project financially feasible. Feeling as though Idaho Power was "the only game in town," the farmers feared they'd be stuck with the bills for the planning and preparation, and they fired John from his position as chairman of the committee.

Certain he was on the right track, and not one to be dissuaded easily, John hopped a plane to New York to talk with investment people at Solomon Brothers. He wanted to find another buyer who was willing to pay the price the farmers needed for their energy.

After some searching, Seattle City Light stepped up to the plate. Eager to purchase additional power, they came to Boise to see the dam and the potential for a power plant for themselves. Knowing that Velma was on the board at MK, John called her to arrange to meet her for lunch and have her help him show the Seattle officials around. She did.

Velma and John Hockberger on their wedding day

The family rode on a wagon to the ceremony

John later wrote her a thank-you note and
sent her a beautiful box of chocolates from
Washington, D.C. She followed up with a
phone call asking him what he was doing that
night. Widowed himself, he answered "not
much," so Velma invited him to dinner. The
East Side Restaurant in Ontario, Oregon pro-
vided both an excellent meal and a long,
leisurely drive for the evening.

Meanwhile, the deal was struck with
Seattle City Light, including a "hell and high
water" clause that John demanded so that the
farmers would be protected during a year
when things might go wrong. Idaho Power
had refused to grant one, but John demanded
it from the Seattle utility because he wanted to

Velma and John

make sure the farmers wouldn't be left with debt and liability issues if there were years of flood or drought.

Velma enjoyed her evening out with John, but she'd been seeing Carly Zell, better known as "Mr. Georgia," and they had been going together for some time. He came to the opening of the Morrison Center with her, they'd been spending holidays together, and she had attended many Washington, D.C., functions with him.

"Suddenly I found myself in something of a pickle. I was going out with John and I was becoming very fond of him. Carly didn't know I'd been seeing John, but John and I were in New York City. We had just checked into the Waldorf Astoria, and we were having a drink at the Bull & Bear when Carly walked in with his entourage. He made a big fuss over me, so John got up and left.

"At that moment, I realized that I was very much in love with Johnny. I'd told him 'you always have a friend with me,' but I realized it had become more than that now, and it was a very touchy thing. I called John at his room, and he said, 'So that's Carly! You'd better just cancel me out and go with him.'"

Velma's heart ached for the man she loved, and she quickly explained to John that he was the one for her.

Not willing to chance losing Velma, John proposed soon after that, and on June 21,1986, the couple was married in a meadow at Jackson Hole, Wyoming, surrounded by their families and friends, with the Tetons rising skyward in the background.

The Tetons were special to both of them. Velma had loved them since she had gone there as a child with her father.

The wedding had a western theme, and the couple and their family members rode to the ceremony in a horse-drawn wagon. The scenery was breathtaking, and they were very much in love.

The only snag in the wedding plans was when the couple realized, shortly before the ceremony, that they'd forgotten to secure the marriage license. A sympathic police officer was nearby, and he offered a police escort to city hall. With lights flashing and sirens screaming, they dashed to the marriage license bureau, arriving with seconds to spare.

Other than the license, everything went as planned. Velma had arranged for two ministers to officiate at the ceremony, just to make sure John couldn't find any loopholes.

Carly finally became reconciled to losing Velma, but she missed his friendship. As time went by, he often invited the Hockbergers to his home, and eventually John and Carly became good friends. "Isn't life strange?" Velma muses.

Chapter Twelve

The Legacy

"Here I grew up a little farm girl, and Mr. Morrison left me a legacy to watch over. He loved the arts, the engineering, the construction. His biggest dream was to bring a performing arts center to the people of Idaho. He reserved twenty acres in the center of Ann Morrison Park for an arts center, but there were two bond issues, one in 1975, another in 1976, and both times the bond issues were turned down."

The second time it was turned down by the slimmest of margins, and Velma was heartbroken. Her friend, Fred Norman, who took her to the airport the day after the issue was defeated the second time said, "The day after the bond was turned down she was at the Boise Airport on her way to Santa Barbara. She was in the process of selling her house in McCall and she was looking at property around Santa Barbara. Velma was despondent and ready to give up on Boise. She was crying her eyes out and felt as though Boise had let her down.

Fred Norman

"She couldn't see any way to make the Morrison Center happen, and she was devastated because it was something she had promised Harry. At the airport, the news people from Channel 2 and the *Idaho Statesman* approached her and were asking questions about the future of the proposed Morrison Center. It was then that the future of the center reached a turning point. Responding to a

Fred and Velma

question about whether the center was turned down twice because it just wasn't the right time or the right thing for Boise, Velma looked directly at the reporters and said, 'The idea of the Morrison Center is too right to be wrong.' Those words became the rallying cry for people with a vision of the arts in Boise's future."

"Fate has a way of improving on ideas," Velma says. "That's how it happened with the performing arts center. That was how it ended up on the campus at Boise State University. In late 1978, John Kaiser, the new president at Boise State, came up with an idea where we created the UCAA, the University Community

Arts Association. That day we met with Ralph Comstock, Edith Miller Klein, Jim Nelson, Bob Krueger and Fred Norman. The organization was officially created in October of that year.

"I realize now it had to be on the campus so it would be available for use by performing arts students.

"After the second time the bond was defeated, I was discouraged and thought about giving up. That was when my dear, faithful friend Fred Norman, stepped up. He directed and produced plays to help pull together funds for the center. Whatever happened, Fred kept his magic wand working.

"John Kaiser was the president of Boise State. The State Board of Education and the Idaho Legislature, through the efforts of my friend, Senator Edith Klein, had appropriated money for a music center at Boise State. Fred, Bob Kreuger, and John Kaiser decided to put the two ideas together. They called it a 'town and gown' plan.

"I thought about it at considerable length," Velma said. "I walked the area and prayed about whether it was the right way to spend the foundation's money. Finally it became clear to me that it was the very thing we should do. It would be built right on the campus for the education and fulfillment of students.

"Fred got a group together," Velma said, "and we went to work. He sent out a call for all who were interested in the proposed center to meet in the ballroom at Boise State

University to discuss a plan. On the way over
he faced his own share of discouragement. 'If
nobody's there, we'll go over to the ice cream
store around the corner and have a cone, then
I'll be off for Arizona State,' Fred told a friend
of his that night. But when they walked into
the ballroom, there were 380 people who
showed up, and we were all ready to dedicate
our efforts to the future of the center."

As they reached the door and saw the
crowd, his friend asked Fred what he was
going to do now. "Ad lib," he said.

"Fred was stunned as he faced the group
and posed the question 'Who wants to be in a
fund-raising production?' All hands went into
the air. 'Honey, what part am I going to play?'
I asked him. Fred said he grew up watching
Vaudeville at the Mosque Theater in Pittsburgh
and his mind flashed back to his childhood.
He looked at me and said, 'You'll be Sophie
Tucker.'

"'But I can't sing,' I told him. 'That's
alright, we'll have you backed up by the
Tuckerettes!'

"At that point, someone from the crowd
shouted, 'It sounds like it will be a Vaudeville
show.' Fred is quick on his feet and he said,
'That's right! It will be called *Vaudeville
Revisited: You ain't seen nothin' yet!*'"

When things were difficult, Velma will tell
you the good Lord sent her what she needed
to find a way to make things work. "Ralph
Comstock was another wonderful person who
came along in my life at just the right time. He

was the CEO of First Security Bank. I knew he was the *only* person who could be the chairman for the building of the Morrison Center.

"I called and made an appointment to see Mr. Comstock. I visited with him and asked him to please be our chairman."

"Oh, my God, girl!" he responded, "I've had bad bank loans, everything is going down, there are many bad farm loans outstanding. I have *no* time to be involved in the center, but I wish you well."

Velma was crushed by his refusal. Her heart was set on having Mr. Comstock head up the project. "In my mind, he was the only one who could pull it off. I wasn't born a Leo for nothing! We don't take 'no' for an answer."

Through the efforts of Fred Norman and Velma, the planning group continued to meet. They were doing plays to help raise funds. Velma made another appointment with Mr. Comstock.

"Velma, I *can't* be involved. I'm just too busy. Things are going on here, and I don't have time. I hear things are going well for you. I hear good things about your plans. I wish you Godspeed, but I can't be involved."

Velma looked him in the eye, "it *has* to be you," she said. "Only you. You *have* to chair the project." Again, he refused.

"It was a sad, sad thing, I thought as I left his office."

Velma began thinking of other people to chair the project. As she leafed through the mental list, she slowly rejected each potential candidate, one by one. There was no doubt that it had to be Ralph Comstock. He was the man for the job, and she was the woman who could talk him into it.

Once again, she called him and made another appointment. "No! Not you again," he shouted when she walked into his office.

"I'm not leaving until you say 'yes,'" she replied.

"You don't know what you're asking," he said, "this is a huge job."

"Yes, I do know what I'm asking," she pressed on, "I know exactly what I'm asking, and you're the only one who can do it." They talked on for some time, Velma every bit as insistent as Ralph was reluctant.

When Ralph finally relented, perhaps deciding it was easier to concede and accept the job than to continue debating the issue with Velma, "I went home and had a great big scotch." So much for the immoveable object! With Edith, Fred Norman, Ralph Comstock and John Kaiser on her team, Velma knew she was finally on the way.

"Our first performance of *Vaudeville Revisited: You Ain't Seen Nothing Yet* opened on January 22, 1981. It was the night that the American hostages were released from Iran. Carolyn Terteling said she thought maybe Fred had personally requested that Ronald Reagan add that little touch for our production. It was a huge success.!"

Betsy Quinn and Velma in her role as "Sophie Tucker" of the Tuckerettes

The Tuckerettes

Even though these are Velma's memoirs, to get the full picture of the evening, I'm going to quote Fred Norman extensively here.

One evening he, Velma and I were visiting about the birth of the center, which Velma sees as the crowning accomplishment of her life. Fred's rendition of events surrounding its arrival includes a more complete picture of the part Velma played in the event, because she's far too modest to take any of the credit for herself.

Fred said, "After the group of three hundred eighty met in the ballroom and we decided on where we were going with it, I sat down and wrote the play in three days, then we

Fundraising for the Morrison Center

Another fundraising production

The Tuckerettes

practiced for months. Our timing was impec-
cable. With the hostages being released that
day, there already was a lot of excitement in
the air. It was at the Red Lion Riverside, and
we had candles with yellow ribbons on the
tables. Velma was fabulous. She and the
Tuckerettes brought down the house.

"Velma was the only person in the show
who was supposed to take a bow. When she
did, everyone in the audience was on their
feet. She didn't take one bow, she took sixteen
of them, and the audience roared. I was in the
wings watching, and I get very keyed up
when I'm directing a production. Finally, I

Velma taking her bows

yelled from behind the scenes, *'someone get her ass out of there.'* That brought down the house.

"At the end of the play is a part where Catherine Elliott was portraying Kate Smith when she sang Irving Berlin's 'God Bless America' in Yankee Stadium in 1939. Before the first note came out, Jack and Esther Simplot stood up holding hands, and instantaneously the audience of seven hundred fifty stood with them. They all held hands and with one voice they sang the song. You couldn't even hear Catherine.

The Tuckerettes

Groundbreaking for the Morrison Center

Velma with Ralph Comstock at the groundbreaking for the Morrison Center. Governor John Evans is in the background.

"Everyone in the cast had tears streaming down their faces," Fred said. "Butch Otter, who played Fred Astaire in the production, said there was more electricity in the room that night than he'd ever felt in his life."

"We raised $9.5 million that night!" Velma announced, then told the cast and audience, "we have our Morrison Center!" She adds, "but, I didn't really take sixteen bows. I was just excited."

That night the audience also listened in on a speakerphone as Velma called Ralph Comstock who was in a hospital suffering from prostate cancer. Weak and in pain, Ralph expressed his disappointment at missing the big opening, but offered his congratulations to the cast and director on the huge success of the event. "You hang in there, girl!" he told Velma emotionally.

"There were so many wonderful people who were part of making the center a reality," Velma says. "We put on plays to make money to build the center: *Side by Side by Sondheim, Oklahoma, Fiddler on the Roof, My Fair Lady, Camelot, Shenandoah, Jacques Brel is Alive and Well and Living in Paris, Man of La Mancha.* It was all local people. My daughter Judy was Golda in Fiddler on the Roof. More than 45,000 came to the performances of *Camelot.*"

Fred said, "When Velma first came to me about the center, she asked me to be her confidante, and she said, 'I want to build the Morrison Center. Would you please help me with this?' I told her it would be my pleasure.

Planning stages

In progress

Grand opening of the Morrison Center

Opening of the Morrison Center

Velma with her hard hat next to the center.

Velma sometimes does this little thing where she's fumbling around like she's not sure what she's doing. Don't be fooled by it. She's like a little fox, and she knows exactly what she's doing. She is a remarkable lady. You don't ever want to bet against her.

"The 'cause' was bigger than the individual, larger than the community, only as big as her heart," Fred said.

"The Morrison Center could never have been built without Fred Norman's guidance and efforts. He worked tirelessly on it," Velma says.

Fred Norman

While each credits the other for the center's success, the bottom line was that the team they put together got the job done.

As the opening performance of *My Fair Lady* played out on the stage of the new Morrison Center, Velma sat back with tears in her eyes, well pleased and very proud. With deep satisfaction in her heart, she knew Harry and his sister Edna would have shared her joy.

The center was the result of the hard work of Fred Norman, Velma, and the dedication of a good many Idahoans who gave their time and money to make it all happen. It was also the result of Harry's and Edna's lifelong dreams, and Velma knew they'd have been pleased to think that Idaho and the world of performing arts would now have an opportunity and the pleasure of becoming better acquainted.

And finally because of the efforts of her friend Fred Norman, the Idaho State Legislature in 1998 officially changed the center's name to the "Velma V. Morrison Center." When it comes to making dreams come true, Fred knew which tugboat worked the hardest.

Chapter Thirteen

A Mother's Tears

Even from her earliest years, Velma knew all too well that, for all the good times and good things that came her way, life had its share of tears. She has suffered more than her fair share of bumps and bruises along the way.

It's hard to imagine anything more painful than losing a child.

Velma lost her younger son, Gary, in the kind of needless tragedy that shakes a mother to the depths of her soul and sends her to storm the heavens, begging an answer to the simple question "Why?" over and over again.

There is no answer except what her faith tells her. Acceptance closed the wound, but the scar never heals.

Nearly forty years and innumerable tears later, Velma still struggles to tell the story of her son Gary's short life and his sad death.

Gary Allan Shannon, four years younger than his brother Ron, was born after the family returned from working the wild harvest. The youngest of Velma's children, he has been described as "a real 'hunk,' and the nicest guy in school," by a former Boise High School classmate and admirer. Through his mother's eyes, he was active and vibrant, a young man who loved sports, hunting and just being outdoors.

When Velma first married Harry Morrison, Ron and Gary were in a military school in California, and her mother and Tom had a home nearby where the boys stayed on weekends. "They made darling little soldiers," Velma said. "Every Friday we would go and watch them march in the afternoon. They would have drills and march all over the fields. It was very precise, and I was very proud of them.

"As soon as we'd pick them up for the weekend, they had go-karts, and they wanted to go out and run them. They did all kinds of races, and that was the highlight of those years. They both did well in school, and they loved their go-karts.

"When they would come home for the summers, we had such good times. We had a boat, and they'd water ski. We'd go up to Lucky Peak on weekends, and they'd ski, have bonfires and we'd all tell stories."

As time went by, her sons spent more time in Idaho, and eventually Gary began attending Boise High School. The family finally built a vacation home in McCall. Velma recalls their favorite times as the snug weekends they spent in McCall during the winter. The boys would be out on the ski hills at

Brundage from the first light until late in the evenings.

"It was always so beautiful. We spent several Christmases at our house in McCall, and it was a winter wonderland. Those were the days when snowmobiles were first introduced, and my boys were wild to get out on them and go exploring. They had the best time out on our snowmobiles."

Then came a weekend in January 1968 when 17-year old Gary and his friend Rick Crabb left for McCall right after school on Friday. Velma's mother and Tom were staying at their Boise home with the boys, but Gary and Rick wanted to be out on their own, so they left for McCall without telling the adults where they were going or asking for permission.

Velma and Harry were in Los Angeles for the weekend, attending a ceremony Morrison-Knudsen called a "pin party." It was a joyous recognition event for long-time MK employees. Harry Morrison personally presented long-time members of the company special lapel pins in recognition of their years of service to the company.

"The boys had told friends at school about their snowmobile trip, but they hadn't told my mother and Tom, and Rick hadn't asked his mother. They didn't want to give anyone a chance to tell them 'no.'"

When Gary didn't show up at home after school, Gladys began calling around to try and find him. Eventually someone who knew about the expedition told her where the boys had gone. Velma's mother, Gladys, and stepfather, Tom drove to McCall, and found that the snowmobiles were gone, but there was no trace of the boys. There was a terrible blizzard going on at the time, and they feared the boys were lost in a storm in the treacherous terrain.

After calling county officials to request help in finding the boys, Gladys called Velma and Harry to apprise them of the situation. As they headed for the airport, Harry alerted the pilots who had the plane ready when they arrived, and they flew directly to McCall. By the time they arrived at the McCall airport, search and rescue teams were already out combing the icy wilderness, looking for the lost boys.

Family and friends of both boys gathered at the Morrison's home in McCall. There were huge bonfires, lots of strong coffee, and the families huddled tensely around radios listening, waiting for any information from the rescue parties searching the nearby mountains.

"It was an eternity. It seemed like forever, but it was only hours. Father Koelsch, from Our Lady of the Lake Catholic Church in McCall, stayed with us and prayed through the night. After hours and hours, the walkie-talkie said they had located one boy, and they were bringing him down to the hospital.

"The families hurried to the cars. We jumped in our Jeep, and went to the hospital, anxiously awaiting the arrival of the search

Gary Allan Shannon

party. The searchers didn't know which of the boys they had found.

"It was my son Gary," Velma says, dissolved in tears at the memory of that horrible night. "He died of exposure and exhaustion. I can't begin to tell you about the pain. No words could ever describe how it felt.

"It was worse for Ricky's mother. Rick wasn't even found that winter. His remains weren't found until the springtime."

The snowmobiles were found parked together under a tree in a steep brushy spot. The machines weren't able to get back up the

Gary in high
school

steep hill they'd come down, and the brush
was too thick for them to keep going forward.
They had lots of gas, but when the boys ran
into problems they set off on foot. "We'll
never know how they got separated, and how
it happened. Children just can't recognize
when they're putting themselves in danger,"
Velma says weeping.

The boys were gone, but the grief over the
loss lingers in their mothers' hearts forever.
There is no way to replace or relieve such
staggering losses.

Second only to the loss of your own child
is seeing your child struggle through unbear-
able heartaches. Velma's beloved daughter,
Judith, also has had more than her share of
tragedy.

Judy fell in love with Bruce Duncan when
they were both students at San Francisco State

Gary with his fiancé, Jody Fretwell

College. Bruce had a good education, and he was from a good family. Eventually they wanted to be married, and plans were being made. They were going to have the wedding at the Palace Hotel in San Francisco.

The Duncans and Morrisons had a small dinner meeting, and both families were agreeable. The date was chosen, invitations were picked out and Judy was in the process of choosing a gown when she called her mother and said to "cancel all the plans."

Stunned, Velma followed her instructions. A month later, Judy called to say she and Bruce had eloped and were married.

It was a financial struggle for the young couple, as they both were still in school, but

Judith Vivian Gatewood

the families finally agreed. The Morrisons paid for Judy's school expenses, the Duncans paid for Bruce's school expenses, and each family paid half of the rent for the couple's apartment.

Things went along happily for the couple for a while. Judy got pregnant, and the families celebrated the anticipated grandchild. As the birth neared, Velma took an MK plane to San Francisco. Bruce was the only family member allowed in the delivery room, so Velma sat in the waiting room by herself waiting for the baby to be born.

Alec was a beautiful baby, and Velma went to their apartment to spruce things up and have the apartment ready for the baby's homecoming. A few months after Alec's birth, however, Bruce decided he didn't want to be a husband or a father, and he moved back home to live with his parents.

Heartbroken, Judy and Alec moved to Boise and found a little house near Velma and Harry's home on Harrison Boulevard. Velma took care of Alec while Judy finished college.

Eventually Judy fell in love again, this time with William Langroise, the son of a Boise attorney, and Velma's heart sang again because Judy was happy.

The Morrisons had a big trip planned to Iran for the dedication of a dam, and Judy was invited to go with them. She had never been overseas before, and she was thrilled at the prospect. Harry's secretary, Petra, arranged for her sister to babysit for Alec, and the group was happily off on the adventure.

While they were at a stopover in Istanbul, Judy received a call. Her fiancé, Bill, and his mother had perished in a house fire back in Boise. Judy was devastated by the news.

Some time later she fell in love again, this time with Herman "Van" Van Elsberg. It was a whirlwind courtship and they were married. Alec was about four-years old when his brother Brad was born. "Brad was a cute little fellow," Velma recalls, "and they seemed to be a very happy family. But things didn't work out in that marriage either, and eventually the couple was divorced.

Judy settled into a life with her two young sons. She was teaching school in California, while her brother Ron had a band that was popular around Boise. Laughing, Velma says years later, Tim Woodward, a band member, recalled, "the Morrisons were very generous about the noise in their garage."

Ted Wilkerson was a member of the band. Judy has a beautiful mezzo soprano voice, so when she was in town, she sang with them. Judy and Ted often played and sang together. They fell in love and were married. Ted moved to California, and Judy was teaching in Pasadena when their son Justin was born.

Judy had taught school for several years when the couple decided to move to Idaho. Ted's band wasn't doing well in California's over-saturated music industry, and they wanted to move back to Melba where they could be near their families.

Sitting, left to right: Brad, Judith, Alec, and Grandma
Lucy. Standing: Velma and her mother, Gladys.

With Judy and the children relocated to Melba, Ted made a flight back to Los Angeles to pick up the last of their belongings and to finish up some appointments. He left one morning, with plans to be back the following night, but on the return trip his plane was struck by a Navy jet and all aboard both aircraft were killed.

"Judy was heartbroken," Velma recalls, overwhelmed with tears of anguish. "There have been so many tragedies for my little girl."

Now a single mother of three, Judy hired attorney Terry Roberts to handle the case of Ted's plane crash. As with all litigation, the case stretched on for years. By the time he had arranged a settlement that would take care of Judy and the three children, they'd grown very fond of each other, and they were married at Harry and Velma's home on Harrison Boulevard before moving to his home in Eagle.

"My heart sang to finally see her happily settled again as a wife and mother," Velma said. But fate had not finished with Judith yet. A few years after they were married, Terry developed serious heart problems. He was hospitalized several times for them, and they were struggling to find something that could be done to help him."

Velma and her elder son, Ron, had taken a trip to Africa to see some of the large ongoing MK projects. "We were gone for several weeks. Terry and Judy and the kids met us at the airport when we came home. Judy invited us for Sunday dinner, and we agreed.

"When we arrived on Sunday, I was helping Judy in the kitchen and Terry was out mowing the lawn. Just as Judy was putting dinner on the table, one of the boys came running into the house crying, 'Mom, Mom… Terry's down.' Judy went running into the back yard to find that he had collapsed at the lawn mower. He died right there in her arms."

Velma wistfully says, "Judy is beautiful and very much an outdoorswoman. She has climbed Mt. Borah, the highest mountain in Idaho, and that is no small feat. She's an avid walker and camper. She is very intellectual, and she reads constantly. She is always a lot of fun, and she has an infectious laugh. Somehow, she has handled the tragedies life has sent her. Hers has not been an easy life, but she faces tragedy with an acceptance that is eloquent.

"Her two older sons, Alec and Brad, each had epilepsy. Alec's was just a tinge, and the doctor said it could be easily controlled with medication, but he wouldn't take it. He was worried about being stigmatized.

"When each of the children graduated from high school, I got them a car. Alec graduated from Pepperdine University. I was so proud. He was so tall and handsome, and he had majored in communications. He moved to Santa Monica, had a wonderful job and he was very well liked in the company. He loved his position.

Alec Duncan

"A couple of times he had severe bruises, but he told fibs to cover for the injuries. Even Judy didn't know he was having seizures. He totaled his car, but covered by saying something was wrong with it, and fortunately no one was hurt in the crash.

"One morning Judy got a call. Alec hadn't been to work in a couple of days, and when friends from work went to check on him, they found he had passed away. It was another heart-wrenching loss for my little girl."

Brad's epileptic seizures were more serious than Alec's, and he conscientiously took his medication. "He was extremely bright in his classes, and a very handsome young man. He truly loved his family, and he was very thoughtful. Brad was the kind of boy who always sent birthday cards and thank-you

Velma with her grandson Alec

Brad Van Elsberg

cards. He was a very kind, outgoing young-
ster.

"Brad lived next door to Judy's condo. At
the time he was going to the University of

Judith's three sons, Brad Van Elsberg, Justin Wilkerson,
and Alec Duncan

California-Santa Barbara. One morning Judy noticed his car was still there at a time he normally would have been gone to school, so she checked on him. He had died from a seizure sometime during the night.

"How hard it is to lose a child. How hard to see your child lose her children. Words have not yet been written to express such a heaviness of heart. It is not an expression."

Velma, Brad, Judith, and Justin at a family party

Chapter Fourteen

Corporate Suicide

During her many years, Velma Morrison has frequently stood triumphantly at the pinnacles of life, and she has survived the valleys of tragedies and disappointments that life distributes with a free hand.

While nothing could compare with some of the personal tragedies she has endured, one chapter of her life that left her with enduring sadness was the death of her beloved Morrison-Knudsen Company. It was a time when Velma, who isn't shy about her feelings on the topic, was forced to watch helplessly as ants callously, systematically dissembled the lifetime of work crafted by a giant. As though watching a Greek tragedy played out on television, Velma stood mute and helpless as she watched Harry's many years of diligence and genius destroyed by greed, arrogance, indifference, and incompetence.

Under the brief but lethal direction of Bill Agee and his hand-picked board of directors, Morrison-Knudsen went from being a renowned, world leader in construction and engineering, to a company that gasped its dying breaths. MK was eventually forced to declared bankruptcy and was sold as salvage to Washington Group International.

"That period was very disturbing to me. My emotions ran wild. I had extensive concerns about what was happening within our corporation. I could see the turn of the tide, but there was no one listening."

Following the death of founder Harry Morrison, Jack Bonny guided MK. Bonny rose through the ranks of the company and served with distinction as Mr. Morrison's handpicked successor. When Bonny retired, another long-time EmKayan, Bertram Perkins, took the helm as CEO.

Perkins was MK president during the Vietnam War. "I'd accompanied him and his wife, Janet, on a trip to Vietnam. It was a strange time. It was during the Cold War, and we had to fly into Russia and pick up a Russian navigator in order to fly into Saigon.

"When we flew into Vietnam, we received a heartwarming welcome from the EmKayans who were working there. I'd been sitting on the MK board before the war started in Vietnam, and there was talk that the war could go on for as much as ten years. I thought that was impossible.

"As it turned out, they were right. Our best talents were in Vietnam for ten years doing jobs for the government and the military. We also built the American embassy in Saigon.

"On this trip, Bert asked what I wanted to see. In Hawaii, after losing my son Gary, I sadly watched many of our young men going through the airport. I'd thought 'how young they are.' I wanted to go to the field hospitals and visit them.

"It was so sad. They are memories that could never be erased from my mind. Even today I often think about that choice. All I can say, now that I am eighty-three and have walked that black granite monument commemorating these boys, is that it was such a waste. A terrible mistake. Our involvement in Vietnam was unforgivable. It was a mistake our president made and the Congress supported. It might be the worst mistake the government has ever made. There are names of fifty-seven thousand men and women etched in that stone of black. For what?

"Bert was a fine man and a wonderful CEO for the company. It was a tragedy when he drowned in the canal near Hillcrest Country Club. We'd been at a gala affair for Fundsy, a charitable auction supporting many non-profit entities within the community. We were putting together money to build the new YMCA in downtown Boise, and this was the first Fundsy that was held.

"We were having a wonderful evening and making money. At the end of the evening, we bid each other good-bye and went our separate ways. Bert was going to Chicago the next day.

"But on the way home he drove into the canal. By the time his body was pulled out of the car, it was too late to revive him. He and Janet had five children. Because of various activities, they had driven to Fundsy in separate cars.

"Grieving, the board got together and chose a new president. William McMurran also was a fine man, and he too had come up through the ranks. He did an excellent job, and he led the corporation well, bringing it into a time of prosperity.

"But once again, fate took a hand and things changed. Mr. McMurran was diagnosed with cancer. He had a fine attitude, and he wanted to beat the cancer. We were devastated when we had to say good-bye. We loved him so much, and he wanted so much to live. He had so much to live for. Cancer took him from us far too soon.

"When we lost William McMurran, I began to see changes within the company. He'd received numerous accolades for his work in construction and business. The Beavers is an old and well-established organization of construction firms. In those days it was 'men only' and the ladies had other activities while the men were meeting. Well, the Beavers had bestowed all kinds of honors and awards on Mr. McMurran, and once there was a formal evening with tuxedoes and a big show in his honor.

"Bill Deasy also had come through the ranks at MK, and he was appointed president and CEO after the death of Mr. McMurran. It was the early eighties, and it was severe economic times for real estate. MK had taken a beating on our many sites all over the country. The interest rates were astronomically high.

"Mr. Deasy inherited the real estate problems. He was capable and diligent, but despite all of his best efforts, things weren't going well. William Douce was a board member. He was the president and CEO of Phillips Petroleum, and he was chairman of the MK compensation committee. That gave him huge power. Bill Agee was serving on the board. Agee was a native Idahoan and former executive for Boise Cascade before he left to head the Bendix Corporation in Detroit. During his years at Bendix, he managed to bring down the entire company. When he arrived in Detroit, Bendix was a large, prosperous firm. Now it no longer exists.

"Well, as the story goes, things weren't going well for Mr. Deasy. The real estate problems were causing gigantic headaches for us. Agee would come up and complain about the problems. He was extremely critical of Deasy's performance. The board was aware of the problems, but many of us were inclined to try and let Mr. Deasy work through them.

"As things kept going from bad to worse, Bill Douse suggested to the board of directors that Mr. Deasy could use some additional expertise to help in the financials. He wanted Agee to serve as a consultant. Mr. Douce called the directors and made a proposal that

Agee would help Mr. Deasy in a consulting capacity.

"Agee said being a consultant wouldn't work, but he would accept the CEO position, and Mr. Deasy could remain with the company as president. There were many conference calls with all of the directors. Later there was an emergency meeting called by Douce. We were asked to vote for Bill Agee to replace Deasy as CEO.

"I remember repeatedly stating my hearty objections. Bill Agee had problems when he was running Boise Cascade, and that was long before the Bendix mess. *'Don't forget Bendix,'* I told the other directors repeatedly. 'It's non-existent today because of Bill Agee.' He still carried the vote.

"I remember this so very well. About two years later Mr. Douce called me personally and apologized over and over, admitting it had been the most drastic mistake to back an individual like Agee to become CEO. Mr. Douse passed away several years later. We had talked and talked, but the company was in difficult circumstances. It seemed to him at the time like it was the only alternative. He had the ultimate responsibility for talking the board into hiring Agee.

"From twenty years down the road, I have to say I still think Mr. Deasy would have managed better on his own. It was just a difficult, strange time."

That, however, is not the end of the Agee story.

"When Agee took over the company, Mr. Deasy was still president. Then I got an emergency call for a board of directors meeting in San Francisco. When we met there, Bill Agee said, 'I cannot work with Bill Deasy. Either he goes or I go.' At that point, we didn't feel like there was anything else we could do. Mr. Deasy got a pink slip.

"By that time, I was getting close to seventy. The company by-laws said when directors turned seventy, they were automatically forced to resign from the board. It was lucky for Agee that I would have to resign because of my age. I'm here to say there would have been hell to pay if I were younger and hadn't had to leave the board.

"The plot thickens as time goes on. Agee paid some of our directors to resign from the board. First to go was Richard H. Vortman, president of National Steel and Shipbulding. Second was Keith Price, the company's executive vice-president. When Agee had Mr. Deasy fired, that took him off the board. Agee's plan was to bring in his own henchmen to sit on the board. The two who left voluntarily were paid handsomely to leave, and it was corporate money that was used to buy them off.

"The first year he brought in Frank M. Adams, Harold W. Andersen, Christopher B. Hemmeter, Donald R. Kayser and Peter Lynch. There were more of his people who were brought in over subsequent years. He stacked the board with people who wouldn't tell him no. No one who opposed him could carry a vote from the board.

"Is there anybody reading this who does not remember the stories about Bill Agee and Mary Cunningham? Their exploits are well known. Why hash it over in my book? Agee was like Napoleon at Waterloo. He had denounced his wife and children to become a Catholic and wed Mary Cunningham. They were married in San Francisco.

"As it happens, Agee went to a Catholic retreat in California. There he met William Clark, who worked for Ronald Reagan's administration. Agee always liked being a big shot and getting acquainted with big names, so he asked Clark to serve on the board of directors. Clark said he'd think it over, and eventually he agreed to serve.

"When he attended the board meetings, Mr. Clark didn't like what he was seeing and hearing. The board was composed entirely of 'yes' men who rubber-stamped whatever Agee wanted to do.

"Clark was given a position on a committee to interview project managers regarding ongoing projects. He announced to Agee that he wanted to visit the sites he'd been assigned to oversee. Agee said, 'don't worry. It's all routine. There's nothing to worry about.'

"Mr. Clark was astonished, and gave Agee the first unequivocal **'NO!'** he'd heard since taking the helm at MK. Agee was taken aback, but he had to furnish the names and locations of the various projects. Clark began

Bill Agee

doing due diligence. He was stunned when
the project managers told him about Agee,
how the corporation's structure was working,
and how things had changed for the worst
since Agee assumed the helm.

"It was Clark who called the next special
emergency meeting of the board of directors
in San Francisco. Agee was not invited for the
meeting. Mr. Clark presented the documenta-
tion of his findings from the project managers
and, to protect itself, the board had no choice
but to demand Agee's resignation. It was
given. Finally!

"Thank God for Mr. Clark! That is where
Agee finally met his Waterloo!"

Nonetheless, it was too late to save
Morrison-Knudsen. The giant had been toppled.

Chapter Fifteen

Friends

"Edith Miller Klein was such a dear friend! She was redheaded, and she had the temper to match. She was the first woman to attend law school at the University of Virginia, and she stood up to the man who tried to shame her by saying that here she was taking a spot that could have belonged to a man.

"She was in the Idaho Legislature, and she was instrumental in helping to make things come together when we were trying to build the Morrison Center. Edith and I were among the first people to visit China after President Richard Nixon visited there in the 1970s, and he talked them into allowing foreigners to visit the country.

"First we went to Hong Kong, and then we flew over to Beijing. When we landed, it was a beautiful sunset, and there was a photo of Mao, about twenty feet tall and fifteen feet wide at the airport. We wanted to laugh, but we didn't right then.

"There were people everywhere, and during Mao's regime, all were dressed in the

Velma and Edith Miller Klein celebrating their birthdays together.

same exact clothing. It was a sea of gray wherever you went. We were very strange to them, and people stared at us in the streets. China had been closed to all foreigners for thirty-five years. They thought we were so interesting. We had taken a Polaroid camera with us, and we took photos of them with us. They were amazed that they could have the photos right away.

"We stayed at the Imperial Hotel. It was not really anything elaborate, but it was very functional. We spent a lot of time walking around the first day, and we couldn't believe how many people there were everywhere, all riding on bicycles.

"The second day we were there we took a train ride to the Great Wall of China. It was a cute little train with four or five cars. There was a woman who went up and down the aisles with an old-fashioned kettle serving tea. The train ride only took an hour, then we got off and walked on the Great Wall of China. It was one of the most remarkable things we'd ever seen. Here I was standing on it after reading about it in books when I was a little girl in grammar school. I actually did have to pinch myself to believe it. We marveled at it, and were overwhelmed at the magnitude of it and the history.

"Edith and I went on a lot of trips together, and we had a good time. My birthday is August first. Hers was the third. We always liked to celebrate them together. On my seventy-fifth birthday, Edith was a few years older than me, we chartered a yacht from Boston Harbor for an excursion, and I took my whole family with me.

"We decided we wanted to see the rocky coast of Maine. We went along for a few days, visiting every little town along the way, shopping and seeing all the handmade wares. After a few days I thought here we were paying for this big yacht and just stopping at little places. I told the captain I wanted to really go someplace. He took me down to the chartroom and we looked over the charts.

"'What's that over there,' I asked him, pointing at the charts, and he told me it was Nova Scotia. 'I want to go there,' I said.

"Oh my word! We went there all right! We had to cross the Bay of Fundy, which has the highest tides in the world. The boat rocked and pitched all night during a torrential storm. Here I had my sister, Melva, my brother Earl, Judith, Ron, Cindy, Drake and my nephew, Frank on board. I kept thinking I was going to drown and wipe out almost my entire family in one outing. I was so frightened. I hadn't seen any life jackets, and we hadn't had any lifeboat drills. I began to realize this captain might not be very experienced.

"I went below. Edith and Melva were wrapped in garbage bags, but they were still soaked. We were so frightened. I went to the captain and asked him about it, and he said, 'This is what you wanted. This is what you get.'

"The next morning we landed at 8 o'clock. We all could have kissed the ground that day! We weren't very anxious to get back on the boat after that, but we did, and on the way back we stopped at Campabello where President Franklin Roosevelt's family had a summer home.

"We two Leos always had a great time together!"

– – – – – – –

"My very best, best friend was Ellen Thurston from Seattle. She and her husband

Velma's mother, Gladys and her stepfather, Tom Neff

Cedrick were the developers of the Western International Hotels. Ellen was a lovely person. She was beautiful and she also was very kind.

"When Harry and I first starting going together, he was taking me around to meet his friends. At that time Ellen and Cedrick owned both the Boise Hotel and the Owyhee Hotel, and they had become close friends of Harry's. We took a trip to Seattle and were invited out on the Thurston's yacht for dinner, cocktails and a cruise of Puget Sound.

"I can tell you that I was very nervous. They met us at the airport and took us to our hotel. Once we were checked into our rooms, they picked us up and took us out on the yacht. Here I was, the little farm girl meeting all of these uppity-up people. Oh! I can tell you I was so nervous, being presented as Mr. Morrison's 'lady friend.'

"First I had a scotch. Then another scotch. Then another scotch. On top of that, I'm not the best sailor. Ellen sensed that I'd had one too many. She let me go back to a cabin to lie down, and I missed dinner. She made arrangements and had a limo take me back to my room at the hotel. The next morning I was still sick, and I missed the customary breakfast I had with Mr. Morrison.

"He called, and said I had to come up and give him his insulin shot. 'I'll be right up,' I told him.

"When I got there, he acted differently than I'd ever seen him before. He was very stern and angry. 'I like you and I think you are wonderful, but we just can't be together because I can't stand a drunk.'

"Well, I was embarrassed and heartbroken. He took me home to San Francisco, and he went home to Boise. I didn't hear from him for a long time.

"Ellen tried to smooth it over. She told him it was the boat and that I had been seasick. He knew better, but Ellen worked it out for me, and he was willing to give me another chance.

"In Seattle, they have a society fundraiser called 'Pancho,' and Ellen was the founder of that. They raised money for all sorts of charitable causes. We took her ideas from Pancho to create 'Fundsy' in Boise.

"Eventually we traveled the world together. We went to many hotel openings. There were some fabulous ones in Thailand and Istanbul.

"Later, when Cedrick passed away, Ellen had total responsibility for the hotels and the company. She traveled constantly, going to openings of new hotels and keeping an eye on the established hotels in the chain. When I wasn't traveling with Mr. Morrison, I often traveled with Ellen.

"Once I took Ellen with me to a horse sale. It was at Hollywood Park, and it was a sale for yearlings. I gave her a list of all of our horses that were going on the block. One of mine didn't have any bids on it, so Ellen bid. 'Sold to the lady in the white fur coat,' the auctioneer called out.

"'What in the world are you going to do with a horse,' I asked her?"

"Nobody was bidding, so I bought it," she laughed.

"'But, what are you going to *do* with it,' I asked again.

"Ellen just laughed. 'Put it under the bed and nobody will notice it,' she said. I don't know what she ever did do with the horse.

"Once we went to the Kentucky Derby together. We had a large group with us, and we were drinking mint juleps and having a great time. We checked into a hotel in Louisville, and made plans to meet at 6 o'clock. As I was getting dressed for dinner, the phone rang. 'What kind of room do you have?' Ellen asked me.

Ellen Thurston with Velma

"'Small!' I told her.

"'Well, I just went into the bathroom and got goosed by the doorknob,' Ellen laughed.

"There was ceiling drywall flaking off and falling on my head during the night. We had made our reservations at the last minute, and they were the only rooms left in Louisville on the busy Derby weekend. They weren't the kind of hotel rooms where Ellen was used to staying.

"Ellen was a wonderful person. We shared great companionship, friendship and love. Her children were my children. My children were hers. She was the friend of a lifetime.

"When Johnny and I were married, Ellen came to our wedding. She said, 'I'll be your chaperone,' and she went with us as far as

Velma and J.R. Simplot

Velma with Ronald Reagan

Denver when we were leaving on our honeymoon. She was heading for Houston, where she was undergoing treatments at the Anderson Center for her cancer.

"We parted at the Denver airport. That was the last time I saw her.

"Life is so sad when you lose your dearest friends. She suffered from cancer. My mother died of cancer. I've lost so many precious friends to cancer."

— — — — — — —

"One of Mr. Morrison's very good friends was Najeeb Halaby, the CEO of Pan American Airlines, and father of Queen Noor of Jordan. Mr. Halaby called and invited Mr. Morrison and me to ride on the first commercial flight

Ron and Velma aboard the first flight of a Boeing 747

Velma with Tennessee Ernie Ford

Velma with Frankie Laine

Velma with Opal Kennedy

Daughter-in-law Cindy Wells, Sally Field, and Velma

Robert Redford, John Kaiser, Cecil Andrus, and Velma

of a Boeing 747. Harry called him back, and Mr. Halaby told him about the size, capacity and range of the newest jet. Harry wasn't able to take time off for the trip, so my son Ron and I decided we'd go on the flight.

"One day Harry's secretary, Petra, called us in Puerta Vallerta to say that the plane was ready to leave the next night on its maiden

Velma with Willie Nelson

flight. It was in mid-December, but Ron and I
hurried to New York for the first flight. We
were picked up from our hotel in buses and
taken to the airport. We boarded in a blizzard.
The plane was called 'The New Miss
America.' My mother saw us on a newscast
and called my sister Melva to watch it also.

"We were all on board and settled in our
seats when they discovered that the hatch
wouldn't close and lock. Back came the buses.

212

We were picked up, taken to a fancy steakhouse, and wined and dined while a new 747 was sent out from White Sands, New Mexico for the flight. I had a few more cocktails, and by that point, I wasn't sure I wanted to go.

"There were protestors lined up by the fence with signs saying things like 'Remember the Titanic,' and I was getting cold feet, but Ron still wanted to go. Out in the middle of the blizzard, a man was painting a sign saying 'The New Miss America' on the side of the new plane.

"Still not sure I wanted to be on board, the captain finally came over the speaker system and said, 'well now, let's see if we can get this hotel up in the air and we'll be on our way.'

"It happened. Suddenly, we were over New York Harbor, watching the Statue of Liberty through the snow, and finally landed safely in London. Buses took us to the Savoy Hotel. It was truly a fun adventure."

– – – – – – –

"One of our favorite friends, and one of my favorite stories, is about Jack Simplot. Surely everyone in Idaho (and most of the world) knows who J.R. Simplot is! He is very dear to us, and he always used to reserve the greenhouse on his estate for us to use before we had our house in McCall. It was a lovely place, and it was used for a scene when they were making the film *Northwest Passage* with Spencer Tracey. Jack was very generous about letting us use it.

"Well, one time when we were invited to Mr. Simplot's estate on Payette Lake, he had a group of bankers as guests. The night we arrived, he announced at dinner that all of us were to be in our saddles at 5:30 a.m., so we could ride to the top of the nearest mountain to see the sunrise.

"We were all there bright and early, and we took off in single file. I was behind Mr. Simplot. It felt wonderful to be out and riding a horse. The morning air was crisp, and the sun was just starting to peek over the hills when his horse started bucking and jumping. He yelled back that there was a swarm of yellow jackets up ahead. I knew I couldn't stay on a horse that was bucking that hard, so I jumped off.

"The yellow jacket swarm moved our way, and I was stung with a vengeance. I was absolutely covered with the stings, and I went into shock. They just threw me over the back of the horse, and I was rushed to the McCall Hospital. Fortunately, they had an antidote and were able to treat me. I was in the hospital for two days. To this day, when I see Mr. Simplot, I always tell him that I'm not going out riding with him again!

– – – – – – –

"My brother Earl and sister Melva have always been such wonderful friends to me. We have shared so much over the years. Melva and I went to Venezuela together when we were young, and we've all gone on all sorts of trips together over the years.

214

Esther and J.R. Simplot at a costume party at the
Morrison's home in McCall

King **Khalid Military City**
WOMENS CLUB
1978 - Saudi Arabia - 1979

We bestow upon Velma Morrison an honorary
membership. Given in recognition for
years of service and dedication to
MORRISON-KNUDSEN COMPANY, INC..

BRENDA REESE- President

PHYLISS RENFRO-2nd Vice Pres.

DOROTHY BREEDLOVE-Vice Pres.

BARBARA BROWN - Secretary

BABETTE FRAZIER - Treasurer

"In 1978 I wanted to visit a large MK project in Saudi Arabia. We were building the King Khalid Military City that served as the headquarters for our soldiers operations during Desert Storm many years later.

"Being a single woman, I was not even allowed to enter the country. Women are nothing there. The only way a woman could enter was if she was on the arm of her husband. Earl had said he would go with me, but even traveling with your brother wasn't good enough. I had to go through Senator Frank Church to get a special permit to travel with my brother.

"The King's City was being built in the interior of the country. After we landed, we traveled to it in a small commuter plane. We could see small families of nomads crossing the desert. There would be a little Toyota pick-up, a small band of sheep, several camels and they were just traveling along from place to place. The women and girls had to walk behind the camels. The boys rode in the pick-ups with their fathers. It was an amazing sight to see.

"The job was being overseen by the Army Corps of Engineers, and the supervisor asked me if I wanted to go out on the desert and collect diamonds. He wasn't kidding. They were not real diamonds, but they were beautiful stones, and they polished up well. He told me to meet him at the pickup at 5 o'clock in the morning and to wear jeans.

"We went out on the desert and he drove several miles out on the sand before he stopped. He said he knew where there were several good spots. He told me to lay on my tummy and watch, that as soon as the sun came up, the stones would sparkle on the ground ahead of me. I just had to creep along the ground and pick them up before the sun got too high.

"I ended up with a little glassful of them in an hour's time. I had them polished in Bangkok, and they are beautiful. I gave one to each member of my family, and kept some for myself. Gathering diamonds on the desert was quite an experience."

As part of her work on the Sansum Clinic, Velma served with Robert C. Van Kampen, who was a lifelong friend of Billy Graham, and the manager of Mr. Graham's personal financial affairs. One day he invited Velma to the opening of the Billy Graham Center at Wheaton University in Illinois. She was overjoyed at the invitation and flew to Chicago for the event. Arriving for the ceremonies on a cold, wet, windy day, the skies cleared and the sun shone as they reached Wheaton University for the outdoor event. Mr. Graham announced that he had talked with the "Man Upstairs" and he'd requested some more congenial weather.

Velma met Billy Graham's wife, Ruth, and his entire family. As they conversed and Velma explained that she was from Idaho, he told her he'd visited Idaho as a young man and commented on the beauty of the state. Velma asked him if he would consider coming to Idaho for a crusade. He checked his schedule and said he would love to do that.

Back home, Velma called together ministers from the local churches and announced that Billy Graham was willing to come out to speak. That was how the Billy Graham Crusade come to be the first event to be held in the brand new Boise State University Pavilion.

Mr. Graham was here for eight days touring, speaking, floating the Boise River and walking the Greenbelt.

Chapter Sixteen

The Bluebird Will Sing Tomorrow

"I started out on a farm that kept our family alive through the Great Depression. Since then I've traveled the entire globe, every continent, and I am always grateful that the good Lord allowed me to be born in this country. Whenever I've traveled, I've always wanted to kiss the ground when I arrive back in the United States. This is a remarkable country. I'm happy to be alive at this time. I've seen amazing changes of all kinds in my lifetime. I've gone from the era of the Model T to watching the space shuttles fly.

"The older I get and the more friends I've lost over the years, the more convinced I am that there is life after death. I've known so many wonderful people, great people. I've seen that the human spirit can conquer anything with the help of God and a refusal to be defeated.

"I believe that we are responsible for helping each other. We should be generous in our words and deeds. God loves the poor and downtrodden. We're all equal in His eyes."

Toward that end, Velma is in the process of having a new shelter home built in Boise for abused women and children. The home, under construction in West Boise is scheduled to open in 2004, and will offer shattered families a safe place to gather their self-esteem and begin rebuilding their lives.

The work of the Morrison Foundation goes on, offering a helping hand to a myriad of projects and good works all over the country. The Velma V. Morrison Center continues to bring world-class performances to the stage for the education and entertainment of Idaho audiences.

"Life is an adventure," Velma says. "I wouldn't have wanted to miss a minute of it. When you reach the twilight of your years and you look back at your life, it goes by in your memory like a river flowing along. Sometimes you hit whitewater and things are very rough for a while, but your faith gives you a sturdy boat to take you safely through the rapids. Then the water quiets and the river flows on to the sea.

"My father knew what he was saying eighty years ago when he used to tell me, 'Codger, when life is its hardest, just watch for the light at the end of the tunnel. The light will show you the way.'"

Scrapbook

Velma with her nephew Frank Windsor in Venice

John and Velma in Perth, Australia. The shirts are from
the recreation of the ship *Endeavor* that Captain Cook
sailed.

Honors from Gonzaga University for Dr. Velma
Morrison, Ph.D.

Velma in Moscow

Oriental Hotel in Bangkok

Velma and John in Australia

In Brazil at Iguasu Falls

Velma in Costa Rica

Costa Rica

Louie Brucker, Melva's husband, with Velma and John
in Paris at the Cathedral of Sacre Coeur.

Velma, John, and Mrs. Derr in Hong Kong.

John in Singapore

Frank Windsor, Drake Shannon, Melva, and Velma in
Florence at "David" by Leonardo da Vinci

Phillipines

Indonesia

Velma and Melva in Monte Carlo

A cancer fundraiser at the McCall Shaver's Market

Velma and her brother Earl

Velma and her sister Melva

Part of Velma's extended family of EmKayans

Retired MK employee picnic

The Board of Directors of National Steel & Shipbuilding which built and furnished the hospital ship *"The Mercy"*. From left: Richard Vortman, Bill Deasey, Velma Morrison, Bill Agee, Bill Gilfillan, Jonathan Scott, Bob McCabe, Bill Douse, Keith Price, Bob Woodhead, Sam Crossland, Harold Stuart, Mike Litterfield.

"The Mercy" was launched on April 4, 1986.

236

The old Morrison Knudsen board; From left: Bob
McCabe, Harold Stuart, Jim Lilly, William McMurran,
Jonathan Scott, Neil Spencer, Velma Morrison, Gene
Armstrong, Bob Woodland

Velma at work on the Morrison Center

Justin and Bonnie Wilkerson with their children Jordan and Janae.

Velma with Michael Landon during the planning stages of the Morrison Center.

Velma with her grandson Drake Shannon. Drake is now
a freshman at Pepperdine University.

Velma and John in Antarctica for Christmas 2001. Velma finally visited every continent on Earth.

With immense gratitude the cast of

"Almost Like a Song...This Moment in Time"
and
The Citizens of Idaho

Celebrates to Honor

Velma V. Morrison

 Valentines Day
February 14, 1998

"From the Heart"

WITH PASSION AND PURPOSE, VELMA V. MORRISON, THROUGH
COURAGE, DIGNITY, GENEROSITY AND WISDOM ALWAYS KNEW
THAT NOTHING MUST SURPASS OUR HUMANITY.

Farewell and Welcome...

Some of Velma's
awards and recognitions include:

- Idaho Statesman's "Distinguished Citizen Award, Nov. 17, 1974
- Pepperdine University Honorary Law Degree, 1980
- College of Idaho, Honorary Doctor of Laws degree, May 30, 1981
- Paul Harris Fellowship Award from the Rotary Club 1982
- Silver Medallion Award, presented on "Velma Morrison Day," by Boise State University, 1984
- Governor's Award for Support of the Arts, 1984
- Inducted into the Morrison Center Hall of Fame, 1984
- Boise Chamber of Commerce "Outstanding Community Service Award," 1984
- March of Dimes "White Rose Award for Outstanding Women," 1988
- Gonzaga University, Honorary Doctor of Letters degree, 1989
- Silver Sage Girl Scout "Women of Today and Tomorrow" Award, 1991
- Velma Morrison Interpretive Center at the World Center for Birds of Prey 1992
- Recipient of the Ralph J. Comstock, Jr. "Light of Philanthropy" Award, 1998
- Inducted into the Idaho Hall of Fame, 2002
- University of Idaho, President's Medallion, 2002
- Member of the "President's Circle" at the College of the Desert in Palm Desert, Calif.

- Listed in the 11th Edition of "Who's Who of American Women"
- Listed in the 6th Edition of the International Register of Profiles
- Rode on board the USS Boise following its christening in Norfolk, Va. by Louise McClure, wife of then-Senator James McClure of Idaho. Also rode aboard the USS Topeka.
- Served as a representative for the U.S. Department of Agriculture to the African state of Kerela

Major Morrison Foundation donations include:

- To the Boy Scounts of America: the land to build Camp Morrison
- To the Sansum Clinic, Santa Barbara, Calif., donation of the Morrison Laboratory, dedicated 1986 in memory of Harry W. Morrison
- Velma Morrison Clock Tower at the (Albertson) College of Idaho, 1990
- Albertson College Endowment Fund honors to: J.R. Simplot, Joe Albertson and Velma Morrison, 1992
- Major Donor: The Community House in Boise, with Michael Hoffman, Fred Norman and Sally Field, "A HAND UP, NOT A HANDOUT"
- West Boise, YMCA, Sept. 1994
- Velma V. Morrison Centennial Plaza at Boise City Hall

- Mission Aviation Fellowship donation for Packer Aircraft that flies missionaries into forgotten parts of the world

Boards:

- Sansum Medical Research Foundation, Santa Barbara Trustee Emeritus
- Trustee, American Council for the Arts, New York & Washington, D.C.
- Boise State University Trustee
- Pepperdine University, California, Trustee, 33 years
- Albertson College of Idaho, Caldwell, 28 years, Trustee Emeritus
- St. Luke's Medical Center, Boise, 25 years as Trustee
- Institute of Critical Care Medicine, Palm Springs, Calif.
- President's Advisory Council for the Kennedy Center
- Boise Philharmonic Association, Advisory Board
- American Red Cross, Board Member
- American Diabetes Association, Board Member
- National Easter Seal Society, Officer and Board Member
- Idaho Public Television, 12 years as Board Member

Some of Velma's favorite scriptures

Romans 8:28   "We know that all things work together for good for those who love God who are called according to His purpose."

Proverbs 3:5   "Trust in the Lord with all thine heart; and lean not unto thine own understanding."

~

Proverbs 3:6   "In all thy ways acknowledge Him, and He shall direct your paths."

~

Psalm 95:2   "Praise God's name. Let us come before His Presence with thanksgiving, and make a joyful noise unto Him."

~

John 14:1   "Let not your heart be troubled: Ye believe in God, believe also in me."

~

John 14:2   "In my Father's house are many mansions. If it were not so, I would have told you. I go to prepare a place for you."

~

John 14:3   "And if I go, I will come again, and receive you unto myself; that where I am, there ye may be also."

~

John 1:5   "The light shines in the darkness, and the darkness did not overcome it."

Treasure in Heaven

Out of this life I shall never take
Things of silver and gold I make.
All that I cherish and hoard away
After I leave, on this earth must stay.

Though I have toiled for a painting rare
To hang on the wall, I must leave it there.
Though I call it mine, and boast its worth
I must give it up when I leave this earth.

All that I gather, and all that I keep
I must leave behind when I fall asleep.
And I often wonder what I shall own
In that other life, when I pass alone.

What shall they find, and what
Shall they see, in the soul that
Answers the call for me.
Shall the Great Judge learn
When my task is through
That my spirit has gathered some riches too?
Or shall at last it be mine to find
That all I'd worked for I'd left behind?